THE ROCKET YEARS

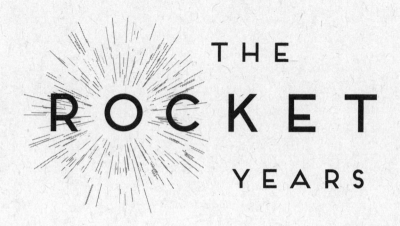

THE
ROCKET
YEARS

*How Your Twenties
Launch the Rest
of Your Life*

ELIZABETH SEGRAN

HARPER

An Imprint of HarperCollinsPublishers

THE ROCKET YEARS. Copyright © 2020 by Elizabeth Segran. All rights reserved. Printed in the United States of America. No part of this book may be used or reproduced in any manner whatsoever without written permission except in the case of brief quotations embodied in critical articles and reviews. For information, address HarperCollins Publishers, 195 Broadway, New York, NY 10007.

HarperCollins books may be purchased for educational, business, or sales promotional use. For information, please email the Special Markets Department at SPsales@harpercollins.com.

FIRST EDITION

Designed by Elina Cohen
(hand high five) Shutterstock / Arizzona Design
(rocket art 1) Shutterstock / Hakki Arsian
(rocket art 2) Shutterstock / Anna Golant

Library of Congress Cataloging-in-Publication Data has been applied for.

ISBN 978-0-06-288356-8

20 21 22 23 24   LSC   10 9 8 7 6 5 4 3 2 1

TO MY FATHER:

YOU SEE, YOU'RE STILL WOVEN
INTO EVERYTHING I AM AND EVERYTHING I DO.
I'LL SEE YOU ON THE OTHER SIDE.

CONTENTS

THE ROCKET YEARS

INTRODUCTION

A few days after my thirty-fourth birthday, at precisely 8:32 p.m. on a Wednesday night, the story of my life crystallized before my eyes.

My husband and I had just spent two hours putting our toddler to sleep. This nightly ritual involved a bath and soapy sing-along, several attempts to tackle Ella and squeeze her into onesie pajamas, reading *Goodnight Moon* fourteen times, then finally rocking her to the *Hamilton* soundtrack until she drifted off. (Even at the age of one, Ella had very specific tastes when it came to bedtime music.)

Ben and I collapsed in exhaustion onto our gray sofa, speckled with the slightest trace of spit-up, and gazed at the living room strewn with stuffed animals, wooden toys, crumbled crackers, and squished blueberries. We turned to each other and burst into laughter at the absurdity of the scene before us. How on earth had we gotten here? As we whispered, so as not to wake Ella, we remarked that it didn't feel like such a long time ago that we had met as college freshmen and proceeded to hurtle through our wild, confusing, marvelous twenties together.

Back then, life seemed so fluid and full of possibility. I saw my twenties as a once-in-a-lifetime opportunity to explore the world, take plenty of risks, and make mistakes. So that was precisely what I did. For me, those years were a whirlwind of impulsively breaking up with boyfriends on street corners, moving across the country on a whim, dancing at block parties till the wee hours of the morning, and spending my meager savings on last-minute backpacking trips to Cambodia and Prague. It was sublime.

I'd assumed that an "exit to adulthood" sign would pop up somewhere in my twenties, pointing me to the moment when my decisions would suddenly matter. But that never happened. In the midst of all that carefree adventure, I made choices that shaped almost every aspect of my present reality. My life as a writer, wife, and mother is the direct result of how I reacted when my dream career went up in flames and my romantic relationships fell apart. And somehow, while I wasn't paying attention, I also built a tribe of friends, formed habits and routines, and cultivated values that will serve me for the rest of my life.

I wish there had been some sort of guidebook to help me navigate the choices that lay before me in those years. It would have been useful to have a map of the decade to spot upcoming forks in the road and "can't miss" attractions along the way. Most of all, I wish I'd had a framework to help me wrestle with the existential questions that occasionally drifted into my mind, catching me by surprise while I was eating sushi with a friend or picking up soap at the drugstore. I remember asking myself: Is there *really* such a thing as a dream job? What about a soul mate? Does my ideal family involve having children? How can I bring my closest friends and favorite pastimes with me into the decades to come? How can I keep my activism and faith alive?

When it came down to it, the real underlying question was this: What will I do with my one wild and precious life?[1] And the corollary: What will it take to create this life I so desperately desire?

On the sofa that night, my conversation with Ben sparked something inside me. I wanted to better understand how one short decade can have such a transformative effect on our whole lives. So I decided to write a book about it. I have spent the last two years revisiting my own twenties, delving into treasure troves of data and scholarship, and consulting with psychologists, sociologists, and other experts. All of that investigation has led to the book you are now holding. In many ways, it's the guidebook I wish I'd had at twenty-two.

Whether you are just about to embark on this magical decade of your life or you're in the thick of it, I wrote this book to help you think more deeply about what you want for your life and plot out how to get there. And if you are, like me, no longer in your twenties, this book is for you, too. I wrote it, in part, because I am interested in where the decisions I made in my twenties will take me as I move into my thirties, forties, and beyond. After all, it is never too late to correct course.

Writing this book has taught me that people's lives don't work out because they do everything right the first time around. People who thrive simply refuse to accept situations that make them miserable: they choose to keep learning, growing, and working toward happiness all their lives. Most importantly, there is no one correct path or definition of success. There is no such thing as wasted time. There is no perfect life. (Nor would you want that; it would be terribly boring!) The research shows us that there are infinite ways to be happy.

This book is about helping you figure out what a meaningful life means to you. Though data helps you evaluate your options, the most valuable data point you have at your fingertips is *you*. In the end, your task is to understand who you are—what you value, what excites you, what brings you joy—so you can map out your own personal itinerary.

PURPOSEFUL EXPLORATION

As I began thinking about my twenties, I came across many ways to make sense of why this decade matters so much. One of my favorites comes from my friend Shilpa Shah, who started a fashion brand called Cuyana. Over dinner one night, she recalled some advice she had received when she was twenty-three and just starting her career. Her mentor at the time, Paul Yanover, told her that life was like a rocket. In your twenties, you are very early in your trajectory, with millions of miles left to go. A few degrees' difference at launch could change where you will land. "When you're young, you want the freedom to make mistakes," Paul told her. "But you also need to think, 'Where am I going?' Do you want Mars, or do you want the Moon?"

The analogy makes sense to me. In our twenties—our "rocket years"—we have more power than ever to chart our course in life and determine where we end up. It's an empowering feeling but also a terrifying one. I imagined my twenties as a kind of playground for me to mess around in before adulthood began. I wasn't entirely wrong; this decade should be about experimenting and taking risks. But the central tension in our twenties is feeling both the freedom to make mistakes and the responsibility to make good choices that will put us on the right track. The truth is that these are not really contradictory: part of the point of exploring is to learn about yourself and the world so you can make the best possible decisions down the line.

Ben, who is a professor of political science, likes to describe the importance of our twenties in a slightly different way. He tells me about the theory of "path dependence," which social scientists use to describe how past choices influence future ones. The idea is that our initial decisions, as random as they are, often have a profound impact on our final outcomes.

There are examples of this all around us. A famous one is the QWERTY keyboard. The first typewriters had keys that were arranged alphabetically, but in 1873, a newspaper editor from Wisconsin found that he kept jamming frequently used letters. One day, he invented the QWERTY configuration to space out the most commonly used keys, hoping to slow down his typing and make his typewriter work better. Today's computers would have no problem with high-speed typing, and, in fact, many of us would prefer to type faster. Yet we're still stuck with the good old QWERTY because it has proven impossible to get users around the world to agree on a new format, then get keyboard manufacturers to make it.

As I think back to my twenties, I recall having a vague sense that my choices would reverberate into my future. Every time I went on a first date or quit yet another job, my mind would project forward, trying to imagine whether I would be happy with that person or that career decades later. The problem was this: I did not have enough self-knowledge to know what I wanted my future to look like. I was trying to chart my course, but I wasn't exactly sure yet whether my final destination was Mars or the moon. Perhaps you've felt like this too.

All of that angst was exacerbated by crushing expectations that weighed on my shoulders. Like many millennials, I had parents who just wanted me to be happy and fulfilled, but I wasn't sure how to make that happen. For instance, my father grew up in a poor family and felt pressure to secure a well-paying job after university. When it came time for me to pick a career, he didn't want me to feel constrained by money but to find work I loved. Even though my father had the kindest intentions, the task of finding a "dream job" felt like a tall order to me. I decided I wanted to become a professor of Indian literature, but after I got my PhD, I applied for every single academic job I was qualified for and not a single one came through. When my career flamed out, I didn't just feel lost; I felt as though I was breaking my father's heart as well.

At times, I felt so overwhelmed and powerless that I would push those decisions aside and distract myself. Sometimes, that meant crawling back into bed with a pint of chocolate ice cream to watch *Pride and Prejudice* on repeat. But other moments called for more drastic measures. The summer I turned twenty-five, when my career and my relationship with Ben simultaneously imploded, I signed up to spend six weeks in a small seaside village in south India called Pondicherry. I was purportedly there to take a language course, but the truth was that I wanted to get away from the choices that lay before me at home.

I spent my days navigating the little town, trying to find the ripest mangoes in the market. I discovered the most delicious okra curry and coconut rice among the food stalls. I got to know the people on my street, such as the chai seller who dispensed steaming cups of sweet tea every morning and the seamstress whose young son played under her sewing table. In India, it was easier to stop fretting about my future and focus on what was in front of me. Escaping felt like a very logical thing to do at the time.

Here's what I have learned: temporarily delaying the decisions looming before me *was* absolutely the right thing to do. As you read this book, it's important to remember that our twenties are not just about making big life decisions; they're also a period of delicious independence. It is the first time we're living apart from our parents, which gives us more control over our lifestyles, and it's before our own family and work responsibilities kick in. For a brief moment, we have the time and just enough money to fill our lives with people and activities that make us happy. This sudden burst of freedom can feel so intoxicating—until it's not.

I spent a lot of my twenties on an emotional roller coaster, feeling liberated one second and burdened the next. (If you find yourself on a similarly bumpy ride, please know it's a completely normal experience!) One moment, I was rushing forward with my life, only to find myself stuck in a holding pattern, going nowhere. I wish I had understood at the time that *both* of these experiences are crucial to making decisions in your rocket years. I see now that my summer in India was not frivolous at all. I needed time alone to grieve the fact that I was never going to become a professor. Far away from my everyday reality in the United States, it was easier for me to imagine myself doing something completely different with my life. I felt as though I was wasting valuable time, but I wasn't; I was dreaming up another future for myself.

If I could do it again, I would have viewed those years as an exercise in purposeful exploration. By this, I mean I would have given myself permission to live impulsively, knowing that periods of wandering are sometimes necessary to figure out who you are and where you want to go. I would have been kinder to myself: rather than regretting each awkward date or career twist, I would have filed away what I learned from those moments and quickly moved on. That slight but meaningful shift in attitude would have let me more fully appreciate—and perhaps even enjoy—each experience as I lived it.

A DATA POINT OF ONE

This book is designed to help guide your own purposeful explorations. It is another source of information in your intelligence-gathering missions.

I lay out the turning points you will encounter in your twenties, offering insights about where each path is likely to lead so you can consider your options. Your biggest, most overwhelming decisions are likely to involve career, romantic relationships, and family. The choices you make in these parts of your life will be deeply personal, extending from your values, desires, and identity. My goal is to help you think through what kind of work and home life will be most satisfying to you, then figure out how to turn your vision into reality.

I also look at other decisions that may seem less consequential at first blush but will play an important role in shaping your day-to-day life for years to come: the friends you make and keep, the passions you pursue in your spare time, and how you stay connected to your body through exercise. And if you're someone with political convictions or religious beliefs, I'll explore how to make them a meaningful part of your life in the decades to come.

The chapters in this book are organized thematically according to three major facets of your life. The first three chapters—on career, hobbies, and fitness—focus on achieving work-life balance. The next three—on marriage, family, and friendship—look at how to build a lifelong network of love and support. And the final two—on politics and faith—are about establishing enduring ties to broader communities.

We're fortunate to be living in an age when we have more access to data than ever before, allowing us to identify fascinating patterns in society. Over the last few decades, researchers have collected and parsed volumes of information about everything from our dating habits to how much we exercise to what goes into a happy marriage. All of this knowledge is powerful. It can help us understand trends and make better decisions.

But data also has plenty of limitations; it can show us correlations only across large populations. Statistics allows us to draw conclusions from the sum of many individual stories, but data cannot capture every detail in any one person's life. And there are always outliers and exceptions to the rule. When you read through the research in these pages, remember that the data do not define you. At every step of the way, you have the ability to change course or defy the odds. If some piece of research troubles you, this is useful information, too. Ask yourself why you are rattled by it and what you can do to push back against the most likely outcomes.

I did this. Medical research has found that there is a window in our late twenties when we tend to form lifelong fitness habits that can extend our life span. I read through those data as a super-unfit thirty-three-year-old and panicked that I had missed the boat. But it wasn't too late for me to get started. In fact, when you take a closer look at the data, they show that age itself is not a barrier to getting fit; it's just that it happens to be easier to form habits earlier in life. That was valuable information for me. It alerted me to the fact that I would have to work harder to get into shape in my midthirties, and it spurred me to join a gym for the very first time. (That yielded some pretty hilarious results, as well as an unfortunate encounter with a treadmill, but more on that later.)

Or take marriage. Recent census data show that people in the United States who get married between the ages of twenty-eight and thirty-two have the lowest divorce rate. This might sound alarming, but remember that the research averaged all marriages recorded in the United States, a data set that included millions of people. There were many people who got married in that window and still got divorced, and there were many others who got married before or after that period and stayed happily married for life. That said, the data do offer clues about what causes divorce. Experts believe that people who get married young sometimes don't have the maturity to deal with the complexity of marriage, while those who wed later in life are sometimes too set in their ways to become part of a couple. Knowing this can be empowering. If you happen to be in one of these categories, you'll be aware of the challenges others similar to you have experienced and can work to overcome them.

YOU WRITE YOUR OWN STORY

A decade ago, when my career and relationship were not working out the way I wanted, I often felt like a stray piece of flotsam in the ocean, flung about by waves I could not control. But looking back, I now see that I was steering the ship, even if it often didn't feel like it. Even when my life felt like a wreck and I didn't want to think about my future, I was subconsciously regrouping and planning the next stage of my life. Even when I stumbled and took wrong turns, I was learning about what really mattered to me, which allowed me to choose what direction to pursue next.

Your twenties will also be chaotic and confusing at times, but know that this is all part of the journey. In the end, you get to chart your own course in life. I hope that reading this book will help you understand and mull over the big decisions before you, so they seem less paralyzing. And perhaps it will even liberate you to enjoy the creative—if somewhat messy—process of writing your own life story.

We are lucky; we have more control over our fates than any other people in history. We get to pick our life partners. We can choose work that not only puts food on the table but gives us meaning. We have more leisure time than previous generations had and can fill it with people and activities that give us joy. All of this choice can feel overwhelming, but it is also a gift.

Now that Ben and I have a mischief-making toddler in tow, my adventures are entirely different from those I had a decade ago. There are fewer all-night block parties or last-minute escapes to seaside towns. But there are new pleasures, too.

I get up at the crack of dawn to sneak in two hours of work before Ella wakes up on a Saturday morning. I take her to a farm to pick strawberries, watching her eyes light up and her little hands get stained with bright red juice. She finds shiny pebbles at a nearby park. We share a chocolate ice cream cone. I fly off for business trips, picking up souvenirs for Ella along the way—a little toy taxi from a New York street seller, an inflatable flamingo from the Palm Springs airport—and hope she doesn't miss me too much while I am gone.

This is the life I have created. I find it glorious in its own way.

ONE

CAREER

It's the night before I am scheduled to teach my very own undergraduate class at the University of California, Berkeley. I'm all of twenty-four, and scanning through the list of nineteen students who have signed up for my class, I realize that some of the upperclassmen are just a smidge younger than I am. I begin to panic ever so slightly.

It's okay, I figure. What I lack in age, I can make up for with some old-school power dressing. I will wear something that projects confidence, seriousness, and authority. This will obviously require a suit. Preferably with shoulder pads. This is an all-important step toward landing my dream job, the one that will get me a paycheck and medical insurance, and you bet I'm taking it seriously. So here I am, standing in front of a full-length mirror, overthinking my outfit.

My roommates are grad students who have already started teaching their own courses, so they kindly agree to offer me sartorial advice. As they're making dinner, I show up in the kitchen in my teal 1980s-style blazer, replete with gold buttons and matching trousers. Alan and Alex laugh me out of the room. They have a point. Berkeley is perhaps the most relaxed research university in the world. It's a place where Nobel laureates teach in cargo shorts and deans show up to meetings in hoodies. "Maybe go for something a tad less, uh, formal?" Alex suggests. He's being nice. What he means is "You look ridiculous. Go back to your room and try again." I settle for jeans and an Oxford shirt.

I really had nothing to worry about. On the first day of class, my students' faces lit up as I walked them through the syllabus. I was teaching a seminar on modern Indian literature that would allow us to wrestle with questions of gender, race, and colonialism. All summer long I had carefully crafted my curriculum. The truth is, I had been preparing for that day for more than a decade. As long as I could remember, all I had wanted to do was teach.

When I was a child, my parents often talked about how powerful education can be. My father was the son of an agricultural laborer in a small village in Malaysia, and he was expected to do similar work when he grew up. Thanks to his intellectual curiosity and perseverance in school, he went to college, then got a job with an airline, where he was eventually tasked with running the company's offices in Brussels, Paris, Jakarta, and London. In my family's lore, education was more than just a bridge out of poverty; it had the power to open your mind to imagine different realities from the one before your eyes.

On career days in school, counselors would ask me to think about my future profession. Perhaps it is no surprise, given my roots, that I picked teaching. As I got older, that vision crystallized into getting a PhD and becoming a professor. It seemed like a career that aligned perfectly with my passions, values, and skills. And I was right. When I began teaching at Berkeley, the experience was everything I'd hoped it would be. I was good at the work. I could see the thousand tiny breakthroughs in my students' minds. I watched their writing improve over the semester. I thought I was fully on track to be a professor in no time.

What I didn't know was that finding a meaningful career is rarely a straightforward path. From the time we are children, we are told to pursue work that we feel passionate about. It is drummed into us that our career should be an expression of our identity and that we should start our search early because it could take us years to find the perfect job. These ideas are powerful; for our generation, a job is no longer just a way to pay the bills but a way to channel who we are and what we value. No wonder so many of us struggle to know what exactly to do with our lives! But even those of us who enter our twenties with a clear career plan never hear about the many things that can get in the way of landing our dream job.

I learned this the hard way. When I began looking for full-time academic work, I discovered that the market for humanities professors was grim. Liberal arts departments had been shrinking for decades, but in the wake of the Great Recession many stopped hiring altogether. I spent three years receiving rejection after rejection before giving up, utterly defeated. After spending decades chasing one dream, I had trouble believing I could be happy doing anything else. It took everything I had to pick myself up and keep searching for something that might make me feel as satisfied and excited.

As I confronted those career setbacks in my twenties, I felt alone. Back then, as I scrolled through friends' Facebook and LinkedIn posts, it looked as though everyone else was blissfully rising through the ranks of their chosen professions. But research by economists suggests that that perception of my peers' success may have been the trick mirror of social media at work; career twists and turns in your rocket years are actually the norm. A lot of us were going through professional turmoil; we were just too embarrassed or depressed to broadcast our struggles to the world.

But I have good news for you: the data reveal that most people will eventually find deeply satisfying work. It just takes longer than you might expect. The road there is almost always filled with wrong turns, detours, and long periods of being stuck in one place, unsure of where to go next. If you persist, though, there's a very good chance that you will nab your dream job.

THE QUEST FOR THE DREAM JOB

Millennials are now the largest generation in the labor force, making up 35 percent of American workers.[1] Gen Z, their slightly younger peers, have begun to enter the labor force and are not too far behind. And these generations are completely transforming humans' relationship with work.

For the first time in history, young workers aren't picking careers based primarily on how much money they will make. This is a sea change from just a generation ago. In workplace surveys, older workers tend to value salary above all other aspects of a job. Yet compensation doesn't even make the top five factors in why today's twentysomethings apply for a position.[2] This might explain why our parents are hell bent on making sure we get a "real" job, while we're far more interested in finding a "dream" job. For our generation, the goal is to find work that closely aligns with our personality, talents, and ideals. The vast majority of millennials (86 percent) would be willing to take a pay cut to work at a company whose mission and values match their own, while only 9 percent of baby boomers would do the same.[3]

In the nineteenth and twentieth centuries, the contract between employer and employee was straightforward: workers exchanged their time, labor, and skills for wages that would pay for a roof over their heads and put food onto the table. But in the twenty-first century, workers expect much more from a job. In surveys, millennials say they want work that is intellectually satisfying and emotionally fulfilling.[4] They want their colleagues to function as a second family.[5] They want their managers to be mentors.[6] Those are a lot of lofty expectations!

Work has morphed from a way to make a living to a way to find meaning, community, and a sense of self. To use the words of *Atlantic* writer Derek Thompson, work has evolved "from a means of material production to a means of identity production."[7] As a result, young people often spend their rocket years single-mindedly focused on their careers. Among older Gen Zers, 95 percent say that "having a job or career they enjoy" is "extremely or very important" to them. This ranked higher than any other priority, including getting married, which weighed in at only 47 percent.[8] That's right: our generation cares more about finding a career than finding love.

We are lucky to live in an age in which work is no longer just a way to pay the bills but can meet deeper existential needs. However, this view of work also has downsides. The pursuit of the dream job can be exhausting and all-consuming. And some young people struggle to find what they are looking for, perhaps because they had such unrealistic expectations in the first place: 71 percent of millennials do not feel engaged at work, which is higher than all other generations.[9] If you find yourself blankly staring at your computer at the office every day, wondering if there is something better for you out there, you're not alone.

The other problem with this philosophy of work is that it blurs the boundaries between your professional and personal lives. Young workers will throw themselves entirely into their jobs and work around the clock because thriving in their careers is fundamental to their feelings of self-worth. Of course, this makes it all too easy for a company to exploit a workforce that isn't as concerned about money by failing to provide livable salaries and benefits. The industries I am most familiar with, academia and journalism, are notorious for doing this. Yet people—like me!—are lining up to do the jobs anyway, because we are so passionate about the work.

Data show that many twentysomethings are overworked, underpaid, and downright miserable at their jobs. A quarter of eighteen- to twenty-five-year-olds reported that they did not use *any* of their paid vacation days in 2016.[10] One study found that more than four in ten millennials don't like the idea of taking time off work, so they're replacing taking vacations with working remotely from another location.[11] Can we stop for a moment to consider how crazy this is? Twentysomethings are working the whole year through without taking a single break! It's a recipe for hating your job and resenting your employer. If I might offer one bit of advice, it is this: For the love of God! Take your vacation days!

All of this is giving rise to a new condition known as "millennial burnout," which refers to being so exhausted from constant work that everyday tasks begin to feel overwhelming. "Why am I burned out?" asked Anne Helen Petersen, who coined the term in her viral 2019 BuzzFeed article. "Because I've internalized the idea that I should be working all the time. Why have I internalized that idea? Because everything and everyone in my life has reinforced it—explicitly and implicitly—since I was young."[12]

How Did We Get Here?

It's worth taking a moment to understand how we arrived at this work culture. Millennials and Gen Zers did not get here on their own. In the ancient world, thinkers from many cultures expressed some form of the idea that you should pursue work that gives you meaning. For instance, the thirteenth century Persian poet Rumi wrote, "Let the beauty of what you love be what you do." The Christian tradition defines a "vocation" as hearing the voice of God himself summoning you to a particular kind of work. (No pressure!)

The ideal of finding meaningful work has existed for centuries, but for most of human history, it was beyond most people's grasp. In preindustrial societies, people were too busy trying to fulfill their most basic needs for food and shelter to find work that satisfied their souls. Workers might have taken pride, even pleasure, in their labor, but work was fundamentally about survival. And our predecessors had little choice in their occupation. Their work was often predetermined: they tilled the family land, took over their family's trade, or sought out work in their village.

Over the last century, everything changed. Modern, industrialized economies created thousands of specialized jobs, enabling people to find work that matched their skills and interests. Workers in developed countries now have an endless number of career options. This new economic landscape has begun to transform the way people think about work. Forty years ago, a new paradigm began to emerge. The organizational psychologist Marsha Sinetar wrote an influential book called *Do What*

You Love, the Money Will Follow: Discovering Your Right Livelihood. Soon after that, everyone from Oprah Winfrey to Tony Robbins to your high school career counselor began asserting that we should love our work.

By the time the millennial and Gen Z generations were born, the idea had fully seeped into the culture. "Do what you love" is the work motto of our time. At WeWork, for instance, you can find the phrase literally woven into the decor, embroidered on throw pillows and adorning coffee mugs. In 2005, the year I graduated from college, Steve Jobs made it the crux of his commencement address at Stanford. "Your work is going to fill a large part of your life," he told the audience. " . . . The only way to be truly satisfied is to do what you believe is great work. And the only way to do great work is to love what you do."[13]

A Healthier Approach

Many people will rush into their rocket years fixated on finding work they love. But in the midst of this striving, most of us don't stop to ask what this really means. Do dream jobs really exist, or are they just a myth? How can you figure out what yours is, and how can you get it? And what does happiness at work really look like?

After digging through heaps of economics research, I have come to the conclusion that it is possible to find deeply satisfying work that aligns with your values and skills. One recent study found that 10 percent of employees say that their overall professional life exceeds their expectations and 38 percent consider their work "awesome" or "great."[14] As workers get older and have more experience, they are even more likely to feel good about their work. (This might help explain why millennials, who are still early in their careers, are less satisfied with their work than older generations.) By the middle of their careers, a third of workers report being emotionally engaged at their jobs, and by the end, this goes up to nearly half.[15] All of this is great news! Many people do seem to find their dream job eventually, and you should do everything you can to be among them.

And if you needed one more reason not to give up, consider how your work can impact your physical and emotional well-being. The American Psychological Association estimated that 550 million workdays are lost each year because of workplace stress.[16] A six-year study found a clear link between workers' happiness and better health; the researchers were able to accurately predict higher blood pressure and cholesterol levels based on an employee happiness survey.[17] (It's official: you can blame your terrible boss for your health problems.)

The big question, then, is how do you figure out what your dream job is? By the time you're in your rocket years, there is a good chance you already have an inkling of what kind of work you would find satisfying. From career day in grade school to picking your major in college, you've been coached to identify your talents and interests. Maybe you've taken a personality test and know your Myers-Briggs Type. You might have already taken premed coursework or done a paralegal internship. You're already on a path.

Throughout your twenties, you will be tasked with testing your assumptions about your ideal career. Until you actually join the labor force, your career ambitions are entirely theoretical. Sure, being a pediatrician may sound great now, but what about three years down the road, when you're buried under a mountain of paperwork instead of high-fiving toddlers at their checkups? You may not actually find your chosen work interesting or meaningful. Or you may discover that your skills aren't a great fit for the job. Or you might confront hurdles outside your control, such as a bad economy or a tough job market in your field. Your company might have unexpected layoffs, or you might be assigned to a bad manager. Any one of these things could torpedo your plans, forcing you to plot out a new itinerary.

These bumps in the road can feel devastating, particularly if you've bet so much of your happiness and identity on one specific career. But the truth is that it takes most workers about a decade to settle into the career they will be in for the long haul. Your twenties will be an extended period of professional exploration. This will sometimes feel turbulent, full of false starts, existential crises, and sleepless nights spent deciding whether to quit a job. But knowing what the typical journey looks like can help you create more realistic and achievable expectations.

One more thing to keep in mind is that even workers who are largely satisfied with their careers don't love every part of their job. Data show that most people take issue with some aspect of their work, from not enjoying particular tasks to wanting a higher salary.[18] As you hunt for your dream job, you should consider which qualities of a job matter to you most and what you're willing to compromise on. And importantly, a job that does not pay a living wage, offer benefits, or give you time off is not, by definition, a "dream job." No matter how thrilling the work, you will never be truly happy with your career if you are overworked or constantly worried about paying your bills.

THE JOB-HOPPING YEARS

After three years of unsuccessfully applying for academic jobs, I gave up on my goal of becoming a professor. I had seen enough of my grad school friends flounder for years without a stable income, taking short-term, poorly paid teaching jobs. I didn't want to waste any more of my twenties searching for a career that simply didn't exist. So there I was, at twenty-seven, without a clue as to what to do next.

Like many of my fellow twentysomethings, I stared out the window and walked around aimlessly for weeks, trying to come up with a new plan for my life. But then it dawned on me: I couldn't figure out my career just by thinking hard; I needed to get up and see what was out there for me. So I began gathering information. I visited more career fairs than I can count. I did informational interviews with anybody who would sit down with me, from management consultants to education policy experts to MBAs. I volunteered at a nonprofit for a few months. I got an internship at a public relations firm. Then I began writing for magazines. In other words, I became a professional job hopper.

Job-hopping is the most common path to finding your dream job. A survey by the Bureau of Labor Statistics found that the average American now approaching retirement age held 11.9 jobs between the ages of eighteen and fifty and worked nearly half of those jobs before the age of twenty-five.[19] If you're in your twenties, there's a good chance you're in full-blown job-hopping mode. Don't worry, this is totally normal. A 2016 survey found that 21 percent of millennials took a new job within the last year and 36 percent said they would look for a new job in the following year if the economy was doing well.[20] Workers between the ages of twenty-five and thirty-four will spend an average of only three years at a single job.[21]

There are many benefits to job-hopping. It allows you to gather knowledge about a variety of career paths quickly. You can acquire particular skills at a company, such as coding, event planning, or budgeting, even though you know you don't want to work in that industry long term. Or you might be excited about some part of a job, such as frequent travel, that you know will be sustainable for only a few years. One of the great frustrations of being new to the workforce is that you need experience to get experience. Job-hopping helps you beat this vicious cycle.

After grad school, I often wondered whether bouncing among jobs was bad for my career. I worried that I might look flighty and unfocused to future employers. But the fact is that employers aren't particularly concerned when an applicant has many jobs on his or her résumé. A survey of three hundred human resource managers found that recruiters begin raising an eyebrow only if a job candidate has changed jobs five times in ten years, which is far above average.[22]

The real question is whether job-hopping can actually get you closer to finding a job you love. The answer to this question is complicated. It depends on a number of factors, including when you do it and whether you are doing it by choice or by necessity.

There has been a lot of economics research on job-hopping. The consensus is that quitting a job to pursue something that would be a better fit is a very sensible thing to do in the early stages of your career. Each new job can get you a step closer to a job that suits you better. Economists also point to other benefits: Job-hopping allows you to gain a wide variety of skills, which makes you more attractive to future employers. It helps you expand your professional network, which can help you land your next job. A job switch also gives you a small salary boost: on average, workers get a pay increase of 3 percent when they take a new job.[23] In your rocket years, when you're likely to move between jobs quickly, those raises add up.

However, the research also shows that around your midthirties, too much job-hopping begins to hurt your long-term career prospects.[24] Over time, changing jobs decreases your ability to deepen your expertise and knowledge. Some skills, such as learning how to use Excel, can be acquired quickly. But others, such as negotiating, mastering a particular kind of writing, or managing other people, take time. And although you may get a small pay increase every time you change jobs, job-hopping too much later on can actually decrease your lifetime earnings. As you develop a clear area of specialization, you become more indispensable, and employers reward that with higher salaries.

Another downside of changing jobs too much is that it creates uncertainty and anxiety. These challenges are easier on younger workers, who are less likely to have major family and financial responsibilities. But if the job-hopping continues through your thirties and forties, it can wear you down psychologically. Another interesting insight is that frequent job-hoppers tend to have more negative attitudes toward whatever job or company they are in at the time.[25] The researchers theorized that people who are always looking for new opportunities elsewhere don't have time to appreciate the positive things about any one job.

What you can take away from this research is that switching jobs can be worthwhile, but it should not be an end in itself. It's a tool. Use the freedom and flexibility of job-hopping to learn about yourself, acquire new skills, and increase your earning power, but know that, over time, the positive effects will begin to lessen. So when you've found something close to your dream job—work that might not be perfect but generally fits with your skills and values—stay in it for a while, deepen your expertise, and rise up through the ranks of your industry.

When Job-Hopping Is Not a Choice

There are times in your career when you have little choice but to job hop. If you're having trouble finding work in your chosen field you might, for example, have to choose a new industry. And starting fresh often means taking a job you are overqualified for. Economists call this being underemployed, which is defined as having more formal education, higher-level skills, or work experience than your job requires. Researchers estimate that, depending on the economy, between 10 and 40 percent of young people in developed countries are underemployed at any given time.[26] That's a lot of unhappy workers. The data show that under-employed people have very low job satisfaction.[27] No kidding! Showing up for a job that feels beneath you is nobody's idea of a satisfying life.

Unfortunately, many people will go through some period of underemployment in their career. I saw this play out in the wake of the Great Recession. My friends and I graduated from college or graduate programs in the late 2000s to find that there were just not enough jobs to go around. Some waited out those years by working as Starbucks baristas or sales assistants at Gap, hoping to find another job down the line. I ended up taking an internship at a PR firm at the age of twenty-seven, PhD in hand. My fellow interns were college seniors. I won't sugarcoat it: I was miserable, but since I could not get an academic job, I had little choice but to start at the bottom in another industry. And I mean the *very* bottom. I spent my days buying lunch for managers five years my junior and cleaning up loathsome spreadsheets.

Social scientists have found that workers are willing to endure this kind of discomfort because it will help them avoid long stretches of unemployment, which can have an even more negative effect on their career. They take low-level jobs to pay the bills and hope that they will be stepping-stones to something better.[28] In some cases, they are right. In the United States, for instance, an economist estimated that each year, 20 percent of workers move from jobs for which they're over-qualified into jobs that are a fair match for their qualifications.[29] But you need to remain vigilant because it is easy to get stuck in an underemployment rut for much longer than you would like. One meta-analysis about underemployment found that taking a job for which you are overqualified sends a negative message to future employers, perhaps unfairly, that you were not smart or skilled enough to get a higher-level job. The same article found that underemployed workers didn't have enough time to properly search for a better job.[30] A medical study found that people who remained underemployed for years were more likely to become clinically depressed.[31]

So what should you do if you can't find a job that fits your qualifications? Economists suggest a two-pronged approach.[32] First, be very selective at the start of your job search. If you can, hold out for a job that takes advantage of your education and skills. Then, if months go by and you still find yourself out of work, take a job you are overqualified for to avoid a prolonged period of unemployment on your résumé. However, it is crucial for you to remain motivated to find a better job throughout this time, even though you might be feeling tired and dejected. This is hard, but it's worthwhile.

If you're job-hopping—whether out of choice or necessity—you need to have faith that you are still on track to finding a dream job. In my experience, glimmers of hope can appear at the most unexpected moments. That happened to me while I was working at the public relations firm. The internship eventually turned into an entry-level job, but it did not take long for me to realize that I would never enjoy the work. I was not passionate about helping midsized tech companies get press coverage. But to do my work well, I had to network with reporters and learn everything there was to know about the media industry; the job was a kind of crash course in the journalism industry. And that's when I had my eureka! moment: I decided I wanted to be a journalist.

It all began to click. My years in academia had trained me to be a strong writer and researcher, skills that are crucial to journalists. I enjoyed storytelling and could write quickly under pressure. I loved delving into obscure but important topics, then introducing them to a wider audience. After three years of aimlessly wandering, I had finally found another career path that I was excited about.

I just had to figure out how to break into the field. I reached out to any reporter who would talk to me to ask for advice. I began tweaking my résumé to highlight how my academic qualifications were transferable to magazine writing. I pitched freelance articles to publications such as *The Nation*, *Foreign Policy*, and *The Atlantic*, and to my surprise, editors were willing to take a chance on me. While still at the PR agency, I began moonlighting as a journalist. I took writing assignments from editors and added each new published story to my portfolio, which I used to snag even more writing jobs. For six months, I spent every single night and weekend working on stories. It was exhausting and I had no social life, but I didn't care. I felt as though I was wasting away at my day job and squandering my talents and qualifications; I believed I had more to offer the world than coffee runs and Excel skills. I needed to get the hell out.

One day, when I was looking at my bank account, I realized that I was earning as much from my writing gigs as from my PR salary, which admittedly wasn't much. It was clear what I had to do: on a Friday in June, I signed up for Obamacare, handed my manager a resignation letter, and kissed public relations good-bye.

LIFE AS A GIG WORKER

Overnight, I became part of a growing army of gig workers. Around the world people are eschewing the traditional nine-to-five office job and striking out on their own as independent workers. These freelancers are all around us: on their laptops at Starbucks, at rented WeWork desks, in their home offices. This new approach to work is variously described as the "gig," "on-demand," or "freelance" economy. And for many people, the flexibility to work anywhere, for as many hours as they like, is the exact definition of a dream job.

An estimated fifty-seven million Americans are self-employed, more than a third of the working population. That's a lot of people delivering food for DoorDash and designing logos on Fiverr. The figure has grown by 7 percent over the last five years, according to a large survey by Upwork, a company that connects freelancers with employers.[33] Every week, Americans spend one billion hours on freelance work, and this number is expected to keep growing. The gig economy is entirely a product of the internet, which has made it easy for employers to post projects and connect with qualified freelancers around the world. These days 64 percent of freelancers find work online.[34]

Young people are more likely to be part of the freelance economy. Nowadays 42 percent of working millennials freelance in some capacity, which is more than any older generation.[35] Their work can take many forms. There are on-demand graphic designers, writers, translators, and web developers. There are freelance lawyers, architects, and marketers. And there are people who work for ride-sharing or food delivery apps. As a result, there's also a lot of variation in how much freelancers earn. The vast majority, 69 percent, make less than $75,000 a year. But 14 percent now make more than $100,000 a year.[36] And remember, some of these freelancers also have other day jobs, which means their total earnings might be even higher. In some cases, the gig life can mean big bucks.

The majority of freelancers—61 percent—work gig jobs by choice rather than from necessity.[37] And it's easy to see why someone might choose this lifestyle. Freelancing offers incredible freedom. It allows you to work anywhere you want, at whatever hours of the day or night, for as long you choose. You don't have a manager who will give you the side-eye if you stumble into work late. There is no organizational chart or fixed path to promotion. You don't have to request time off months in advance. Half of freelancers say that no amount of money would convince them to take on a traditional job. And 42 percent of people say that freelancing gives them the ability to make money even though they are unable to work for a regular employer due to personal circumstances, such as health issues or looking after their children.

However, it's not all rosy. The gig economy has also created a lot of low-paying work, mostly in the form of on-demand jobs with startups such as Uber, Seamless, and TaskRabbit. These companies promise workers flexible work arrangements, so they can earn extra cash in their spare time. But many people now rely on gig work for their entire income. This is a problem because these jobs don't come with benefits or stability. Deloitte found that back in 2003, gig workers generated 57 percent of their total income from on-demand jobs, but by 2015, 72 percent of their income came from this kind of work.[38] The data show that twentysomethings in the gig economy consistently make less money than their peers who are working full-time jobs. In 2013, millennial gig workers made an average of $38,000 a year, compared to the more than $40,000 made by their counterparts with traditional jobs.[39]

So how can you tell if freelancing is for you? To start with, you need to consider your motivations. If you're looking to earn extra cash while figuring out your next career move, gig work can relieve some financial pressure. If you're sending out your résumé but no employers are biting, driving for Lyft might enable you to pay your bills while you hold out for the job you really want. But much like being underemployed, you need to be careful not to get so absorbed by your gig that you don't have time to pursue a career you are really passionate about.

On the other hand, perhaps you're thinking about making gig work a full-time career. Rather than working for a single company, you're excited about applying your skills and education to doing project work for multiple employers. The best way to tell if this lifestyle will work for you comes down to your personality. When you examine the data on the gig economy, it is clear that the workers who most enjoy this kind of work prioritize freedom over stability and are good at organizing their time and money.[40] These are people who bristle at the idea of a boss breathing down their necks, hate clocking in at an office, and dream of working remotely from a beach in Hawaii. They aren't focused on earning an enormous salary; some freelancers do, but they're rare. They don't mind the ongoing process of pitching new clients and don't panic during times when no work seems to be coming in.

In the year I was a full-time gig worker, I saw the positives and negatives of freelancing up close. Since I was just starting my career as a journalist, it was valuable to write for many magazines: I got to work with different editors, explore various types of writing, and glimpse the cultures at each workplace. I enjoyed working from my dining table or my neighborhood coffee shop. Some days I would work late into the night and then sleep in or take an afternoon off to watch a movie.

But freelancing came with some anxieties. Finding medical insurance was a nightmare: I spent weeks parsing every inch of fine print on the Obamacare website. Instead of receiving a monthly paycheck, money would trickle into my bank account at irregular intervals. My workload varied throughout the year. In the fall, I locked down many assignments, but during the summer and winter holidays, when editors went on vacation, I would struggle to find a single one. That meant creating a monthly spending budget and putting aside money for lean seasons. And of course, freelancers don't get paid time off. I took one weeklong holiday during the entire period I was a gig worker. Not only did I have to save carefully for the trip, I knew I would not earn any money during my time away. And I had to set aside my worry that by committing to the vacation, I might be giving up a lucrative assignment that had yet to materialize.

Gig workers have mixed feelings about their lifestyle. Upwork's survey showed that 63 percent of full-time freelancers feel anxious about all they have to manage, even though 77 percent say that this lifestyle gives them better work-life balance.[41] For an increasing proportion of workers, freelancing will be a lifelong career. But for others, it might just be another stop on the road to a more traditional job.

I fell into the latter category. I loved being a gig worker, but I reached a turning point when Ben and I decided to have a baby. It was stressful enough managing my finances as a childless freelancer, but adding pregnancy and maternity leave to the mix seemed more than I could handle. When the instability of freelancing started to feel overwhelming, I began looking for more permanent work. One day, an editor at *Fast Company* told me that a full-time staff writer position had opened up. Based on the many stories I had already written for the magazine, she said it was keen to hire me. I could even keep working from home, if I wanted. I said "yes" on the spot.

By the time I turned thirty, my job-hopping, gig-working days were over. After years of searching, I was finally doing work I enjoyed and found meaningful. It paid well and came with both benefits and time off. *Fast Company* sent me a box of business cards in the mail that declared my new identity: I was now a magazine writer. I've now been at this job for five years, and I still love the work. My daily routine involves cranking out stories on all kinds of topics, from fashion trends to climate change to futuristic handbags. I travel frequently to report stories and moderate panels, hopping from New York to Milan to San Francisco in any given week.

My quest to find my dream job is over. I have found it, and the task at hand is to do it well.

SHOULD YOU GET MORE EDUCATION?

Of all the questionable professional decisions I made in my twenties, one in particular stands out: going to graduate school. I take comfort in the fact that I'm not alone—nearly two million people are enrolled in graduate programs every year[42]—but it is hard not to wonder whether it was worth spending six years and who knows how much in forgone earnings working toward an academic job that never materialized.

I went directly from college into a PhD program, thinking it would be my path to a long, fulfilling career as a professor.

People warned me that going into academia would be an uphill battle, but I didn't want to believe them. If anyone could snag a professorship, it would be me! Surely my passion and determination would empower me to barrel through the terrible odds.

I was wrong. If I had taken a moment to look through the numbers, it would have been clear that my persistence was no match for the dire academic job market. The percentage of PhDs that have gotten academic jobs has hovered around 20 percent for the past forty years.[43] Nearly half of PhDs graduate without any job lined up at all, whether in academia or elsewhere.[44] I doubt that those figures would have compelled me to abandon my quest to become a professor. But I would have gone into my program with my eyes open. I might have come up with a Plan B earlier or done an internship outside academia. I would not have been quite so shocked when I sent out eighty job applications a year for three years and none yielded a job.

My story serves as a cautionary tale. It's easy to get swept away by the idea that further education will fast-track you to your dream job. If you're thinking about getting an advanced degree, take the time to consider your options and the most likely outcomes. For some people, an advanced degree or a certificate program is a ticket to a higher-paying position that perfectly aligns with their passions or an opportunity to switch careers when they realize they got off to a wrong start. For instance, consulting firms sometimes require an MBA to get promoted, you need a JD to become a lawyer, and you need certifications to teach in some schools. But others find that their additional qualification does not lead to better work. Instead, it saddles them with crushing debt, forcing them to take any job they can to pay it off. The devil is in the details: your chances of success depend on the program, the institution, and the state of the job market.

Americans are now more educated than ever before. Twenty-one percent of the population has at least a college degree, and an additional 12 percent has an advanced degree.[45] Since 2000, the percentage of Americans with advanced degrees has almost doubled.[46] Doctorates are rare, making up 1 percent of the population, but a master's has been a hot commodity for about a decade, with 9 percent of Americans holding one.[47] And these degrees span the gamut from business administration to architecture to software engineering to public health to fine arts to divinity, each yielding wildly different career paths. "Call it credential inflation," declared the *New York Times* back in 2011. "Once derided as the consolation prize for failing to finish a Ph.D. or just a way to kill time waiting out economic downturns, the master's is now the fastest-growing degree."[48]

Advanced degrees come at a hefty price. If you get a PhD, you will probably not have to shell out a lot of money for it. Most universities ask doctoral students to teach in exchange for covering their tuition and living expenses. But these degrees take a long time to earn, which means that you must consider your opportunity costs. It takes 8.2 years on average to get a doctorate, and the average student is thirty-three years old when he or she graduates. Those years could have been spent earning money in the job market. And as I learned, if you cannot get an academic job in your highly specialized field, it is very hard to transition into another industry.

Master's degrees are a different story. It takes two to three years to complete a master's degree, but it costs an average of $24,812 a year in tuition out of pocket.[49] At more prestigious institutions and in lucrative fields, you can expect to pay double that or more. That's the cost of a wedding and a down payment on a house. Three-fifths of those with a master's degree leave with debt that commonly runs into the tens of thousands of dollars.[50] The vast majority of people working toward a master's—90 percent—believe that the degree will lead to increased earnings, which is perhaps why 86 percent of them say that cost was not a factor when they made the decision.

There is also the option of a graduate certificate, sometimes known as a diploma, in a more specialized field such as accounting, computer science, or supply chain management. More than half of those with advanced education have a diploma, sometimes in addition to another degree.[51] These programs tend to be shorter, consisting of fewer than seven courses in your area of concentration, and take about a year. These programs have become increasingly popular in recent years, partly because they require half the time and money of a master's degree.[52] However, they tend to be more focused, so you will need to be sure about the career path you want to take and even the subfield you want to become an expert in. If you end up changing your mind about what you want to do, a diploma is less likely to be transferable.

It's true that advanced degrees generally result in higher earnings. In 2015, the mean earnings of thirty-five- to forty-four-year-olds with master's degrees were 23 percent higher than those with bachelor's degrees ($87,320 versus $71,100).[53] But whether that salary bump is worth it depends on how much you paid for the degree. In a Gallup survey of more than four thousand people who received a master's degree or higher between 2000 and 2015, more than half of people with a master of science or master of arts said that grad school was not worth the price tag. Even in fields that seem to have a big payoff, people were dissatisfied: 77 percent of those with law degrees, 56 percent of those with MBAs, and 42 percent of those with medical degrees said that grad school was not worth the cost.

Did the additional education actually prepare them for their careers? Half of those with medical degrees said no. And among those with a law degree, MBA, master of science, or master of arts, 70 percent or more said that grad school was not good training.[54] These statistics aren't encouraging. Yet the flip side is that there were many people who were very satisfied with their advanced degree.

It is tempting to treat graduate school as another form of career exploration, but the data suggest that this is a bad idea: 26 percent of people who start a master's program quit before getting their degree, realizing that it wasn't the right track for them. Many paid thousands of dollars in tuition with nothing to show for it.[55] If you're still figuring out what kind of work you enjoy, it makes sense to job hop a few more years, to better understand what you really want from your career.

People flock to grad school when the economy is bad. This is risky. During the Great Recession, the number of students applying to grad schools jumped by more than 8 percent each year. Yet when they completed their graduate programs, companies were still not hiring and salaries remained depressed. Between 2008 and 2011, the number of newly minted lawyers who got legal jobs dropped from 74 percent to less than 60 percent.[56] And those who didn't get hired still had an average of $125,000 in law school debt.

On the other hand, once you're sure about the job you really want, you might discover that there are credentials, practical skills, or paper qualifications you need to move forward. In some cases, you might just need to take a specialized course or two from a university extension program or a coding boot camp such as General Assembly or Flatiron School. In other cases, getting an advanced degree or diploma might be the right move.

If you *are* considering graduate school, get as much data as you can about each individual program you're considering. Don't rely on general industrywide data about salaries and career outcomes. In many fields, graduates from top-ranked institutions have very different career trajectories from those in lower-ranked ones. In one study, MBAs at the top ten business schools, for example, had starting salaries of between $161,078 and $176,705, while those in the lower half of the top fifty did not break $100,000.[57] Yet even poorly ranked business schools charge hefty tuition fees totaling well into six figures. Most universities have very detailed information about students' outcomes, including typical jobs, starting salaries, and how long it takes the average student to find a job. Ask to see the latest statistics. If I had gone to my department at Berkeley before matriculating, the dean could have told me that the vast majority of graduates in my field did not become professors, which would have informed my decision.

Given the high price of graduate school, money is inevitably an important consideration. Taking out a big loan to get an advanced degree can narrow your career options down the road, because you'll have to prioritize compensation once you're back on the job market again. But there are also intangible things you get from a graduate program that cannot be quantified. You'll have valuable time to learn about things you care about. You'll meet like-minded people who could become lifelong friends. You'll be able to take a break from working, think deeply, perhaps even travel. These are worth factoring into your decision.

To be clear, I don't regret getting my PhD. Those years were among the best of my life. I've never been happier than when I was in a Berkeley classroom a decade ago, introducing students to my favorite authors. I spent my summers traveling through Indian towns. I translated ancient poetry, making it accessible to a new audience of English speakers. Those were all worthwhile endeavors. And I did not leave with debt, which gave me the freedom to seek another meaningful, enjoyable job—one I had never considered before because I had been too busy annotating poems under a tree on campus.

All of that led me here, to my life as a writer. Now that I'm in my thirties, my career has settled into a rhythm. I have a home office, so my daily commute from my bed to my desk in the attic takes about ten seconds. On a typical workday, I get up very early—a little after 5:00 a.m.—sip my coffee, and work for two hours while the rest of my family is still fast asleep. When Ella wakes up at around 7:00 a.m., we play together and read books before I get her dressed for school. Then the two of us go down to the kitchen, where Ella eats her breakfast with the same five *Sesame Street* songs playing in the background, while I pack her lunch box. After Ben and Ella drive off for the day, I go back upstairs to work.

I took a long, meandering road to my dream job. But all those false starts and detours led me right here, to this desk, where I spend my days typing away in my polka-dot pajamas and fluffy slippers while watching the sun come up outside my window. It's not what twenty-four-year-old me planned, but I can't imagine a happier life. And there's not a teal blazer or shoulder pad in sight.

TWO

HOBBIES

On our third day in Cambodia, I decided to take a little trip by myself to Oudong, a mountaintop temple an hour's drive from Phnom Penh, the city where we were staying. My guidebook said that it was a bit of a trek but the views from Oudong's peak were well worth it. Of course, I didn't have a car, and I couldn't afford a taxi on my shoestring budget. So I figured I would just travel there by *tuk-tuk*, a local vehicle that is basically a motor-cycle with a seat jerry-rigged to the back.

My friend Kate and I had come to Cambodia on a whim in the summer of 2007, the year I turned twenty-four. A buddy of Kate's worked for a nonprofit in Phnom Penh and had invited us to come visit. At the time, Kate was waitressing and I was a grad student, but we somehow thought it would be a good idea to pour our meager savings into a trip through Southeast Asia. We quickly sketched out a plan that would take us from Bangkok to Phnom Penh to Siem Reap, where we would see the Angkor Wat temple, one of the seven wonders of the ancient world. But looking back at the trip many years later, it was my solo journey to Oudong that stands out in my mind: in that moment, I discovered my desire to take in as much of the world as I could in my lifetime. I would devote my twenties to fulfilling that wish. And travel would become an enduring passion.

While Kate spent the day catching up with her friend, I asked our hostel if they could recommend a reliable *tuk-tuk* driver. A few hours later, I found myself chugging along a dusty village road. My driver and I sat in amicable silence, not knowing each other's language. As cars and buses whizzed past us, I began to realize that it was going to take twice the time my guidebook estimated to get to the mountain, since nobody in her right mind does the journey on a *tuk-tuk*. On the other hand, because these vehicles have no windows—just a little flap of clear plastic on each side in case of rain—I could observe everything around me.

Stuck in Phnom Penh traffic, I could smell the freshly baked baguette loaves that bakers were delivering to restaurants, a legacy of the years when Cambodia was a French colony. At one point, the *tuk-tuk* was dwarfed by a trainer guiding his elephant on a leisurely stroll down the street. Since elephants are considered lucky in these parts, passersby would pay to have the elephant bless them, which amounted to having the creature bonk them on the head with its trunk. Then, moments later, the countryside opened up to us, with paddy fields in every direction and farmers bundling bales of rice. I could smell the mud and water buffaloes just feet away.

The driver dropped me off at the foot of the mountain. In the afternoon heat, I began scaling the five hundred steps to get to its peak. The whole temple complex was eerily quiet, except for the occasional rustle of monkeys scurrying among the trees of the surrounding jungle. There were no other tourists in sight, but every so often a young monk in saffron robes would come into view at the top. As I ascended, I began to discern a sound like nothing I had ever heard before. In a dark pavilion, two dozen monks, from teenagers to old men, were performing a low, guttural chant. It was both spine chilling and tranquil. In the distance, through a window, all you could see was clear blue sky. It was the closest thing to Heaven I could imagine.

I found it hard to put the experience into words when I told Kate all about it over fish curry and rice at dinner that night. There would be many other memorable moments on that trip, but being on that mountain surrounded by meditating monks will stay forever etched in my memory. Though many of the monks had witnessed horrific tragedies in their country during their lifetimes, they had somehow found a source of inner peace.

That trip to Cambodia marked a turning point in my life. After that, all I wanted to do was see remote corners of the planet and understand how people there lived and saw the world. Throughout my twenties, I took a trip whenever I had the time or money to spare. I backpacked through Indonesia with my friend Isabel, staying in hostels usually reserved for truck drivers. One winter, Kate and I found a cheap airline ticket to the Czech Republic, where we feasted on dumplings for days. Traveling became a bit of a drug for me: I got an adrenaline rush every time I stepped off a flight or train in a new place. I loved the sensory overload of the heat against my skin, the spices wafting from the street stalls, and the buzz of people hitching rides on auto rickshaws and bullock carts.

I did not pick up many hobbies in my rocket years, but I am grateful that travel was one of them. It is one of the few deeply satisfying activities outside of work and family that I have brought with me into my thirties. These days, I barely have any free time at all: I spend my weekends shuttling Ella to playdates and music classes, getting in some work on my book or articles I didn't finish the previous week, then prepping meals and doing laundry for the following week. There are many hobbies I wish I could incorporate into my life, such as going on long bike rides in Boston, but I just don't have the bandwidth to get started.

Yet I always make travel a priority. Every year, I save up money and vacation time to visit a new place. If I can't find anyone to go with me, I travel by myself. I do this partly because planning trips, hopping on a plane, and navigating foreign places are second nature to me by now, so they don't require much mental effort even when I feel stretched thin. But perhaps more important, traveling enables me to tap into parts of my identity I don't get to experience much in everyday life. It allows me to remember who I was before I became a journalist or a mother.

WHY HOBBIES MATTER

The word *hobby* has always sounded a little old-fashioned to me. It conjures up memories of my fifth-grade teacher, Miss Alice, who encouraged my classmates and me to stay out of trouble by throwing ourselves into good, clean pastimes. Her suggested hobbies? Stamp collecting or embroidery. (We loved her dearly, but, as preteens glued to our Game Boys, our response was a collective eye roll.) But now I wish I had not been so quick to dismiss the concept. As I researched this chapter, I began to see that hobbies—which are defined as the activities you do for pleasure in your leisure time—are a powerful way to stay connected to your passions throughout your life.

Hobby scholars (yes, that's a thing) say that hobbies have a way of shaping and reinforcing our identities, which is something I have found to be true in my own life.[1] We sometimes seek out hobbies that reflect our values and our sense of self, whether we think we're sporty or musical. But we occasionally stumble into hobbies entirely by chance and discover a new passion. A friend might take you on a hiking trip and turn you into an outdoorsy type; attending a comic convention might get you interested in cosplay. The hobbies we settle on, as random as they are, end up defining us.

Like most people, I spent my twenties focused on what I believed to be the three most important areas of my life: career, marriage, and family. But scholars point out that besides being enjoyable, hobbies can also enhance these other aspects of your life. Lots of research shows that spending time on hobbies is good for your mind and body: people with hobbies tend to be less depressed, have better cardiovascular health, and show more interest in the world around them, which is a marker of good mental health.[2] A 2015 medical study suggested that hobbies could be an intervention for improving health and well-being in daily life, after finding that people who practiced them experienced more happiness and less stress.[3] (Skip the CBD! Knit a sweater instead!) All of this translates into improving your day-to-day life in tangible ways. Your hobbies allow you to cultivate parts of your identity outside of your close relationships, which puts less pressure on your friends and family to be essential to your happiness. When your work gets stressful, having interests outside your job provides a healthy outlet for your anxiety. In other words, hobbies give you a more balanced perspective on the world, which can help you be a better partner, parent, or employee. Who knew you could get so much from hiking or singing in the choir every weekend?

There's a lot of variation in how people incorporate hobbies into their lives. Surveys have found that 20 percent of the population have no hobbies at all. A quarter has a single hobby they practice regularly. And a little over half the population has multiple hobbies.[4]

These days, there are as many different hobbies as there are people in the world. When the Bureau of Labor Statistics tracked the activities Americans pursued in their leisure time, they spanned the gamut, including everything from sports such as golf, softball, and basketball; working out, lifting weights, dancing, and attending fitness classes; hunting and hiking; playing video games and board games; reading, watching movies, visiting museums, and attending concerts; doing crafts, building things, writing for pleasure, and playing music; and, of course, watching television.[5] All of this shows that hobbies are, in many ways, a form of self-expression: they allow you to explore your own interests, but they also telegraph those interests to the rest of the world.

Research also shows that most of us pick up our hobbies in a narrow window of time. In general, we seem to settle into our lifelong hobbies in our twenties, and as we move into our thirties, we are likely to fall back into hobbies that we are already familiar with. This means that if you don't make a conscious effort to explore new hobbies, you aren't likely to pick up new ones after your rocket years—and you may even struggle to find time to do the ones that you already love.

Knowing the trends can empower you to buck them. The research can nudge us to be more deliberate about exploring new activities in our twenties and developing the skills necessary to bring them with us into subsequent decades. Later in this chapter, I will lay out some strategies for cultivating hobbies throughout your life and coping with the challenges of picking up new hobbies as you get older. But before that, it's valuable to understand why it is worth thinking about how you spend your leisure time in your twenties, when you have the time and energy to explore your passions.

WHY YOU SHOULD INVEST IN HOBBIES
IN YOUR TWENTIES

Hobbies aren't merely a way to fill our leisure hours; since we tend to pick hobbies that are deeply intertwined with our identities and personalities, they seem to be a way for us to hold on to our sense of self as time passes and our lives change. And in old age, hobbies seem to be a way to stay connected to the people we were when we were just starting out in life.

In one study, scholars tracked a panel of 495 people over the course of thirty-four years. They found that people's hobbies in old age (between sixty-six and eighty-nine) were almost identical to their hobbies at the start of the experiment. People in their eighties who spent their leisure time gardening or reading or visiting restaurants had, in fact, been pursuing the same hobbies their entire lives.[6] There were a couple of exceptions; a few older people took up things such as square dancing because classes were offered in retirement homes. But for the most part, older people tended to pursue the hobbies of their youth and gave them up only when they were physically unable to continue doing them. The researchers found that people who loved fishing, for instance, stopped fishing only in their seventies, when various infirmities kicked in.

One school of psychology makes the case that pursuing the same hobbies over the course of our lifetimes is a coping mechanism to deal with the challenges of aging, including losing your social status and confronting the death of your friends and relatives. George Maddox and Robert Atchley observed that older adults show a lot of consistency in their behaviors, particularly their leisure activities, even as their bodies and minds deteriorate. They developed the "continuity theory of aging," which theorized that people adapt to the changes that come with getting older by focusing on the behaviors and activities they did in the past.[7]

In the current context, one way to figure out when people pick up hobbies is through their online browsing habits. The internet is a valuable resource for people to learn about new hobbies and develop the skills necessary to practice them. YouTube is full of videos that teach you how to play an instrument, crochet, or hold a tennis racket.

Ben ran an experiment to better understand when in life people tend to pick up hobbies. He gathered the anonymized browsing data of over eighty thousand households, representing a cross section of the population, through a platform called Comscore. He then mapped out how much time those people spent on the top fifty websites within each category of leisure activity, including sports, art, music, travel, collecting, and crafts, as determined by a web-ranking service called Alexa. He found that people in their twenties are more likely to spend time online learning about hobbies than are those in older age groups. People in their twenties spend about 1 percent of their total time online on hobby-related websites, but the share of time people in their thirties spend on hobby websites is half that. Based on current estimates about how much time the average person spends online, this would suggest that a twentysomething spends 934 minutes per year on hobby-related websites, as opposed to 588.5 minutes per year for those who are older.[8]

Why are we less inclined to pick up hobbies as we get older? For one thing, doing a hobby often requires developing an entirely new skill set. Although we pursue hobbies for fun, they usually require some level of skill that takes time and energy to learn. Hobby scholars point out that one person's hobby, such as fixing cars or baking, might be another person's job.

The hobbies I pursued in my twenties certainly involved a steep learning curve. When I think back to my trip to Oudong, I realize I was gathering valuable lessons about how to plan itineraries, manage travel logistics, find authentic local cuisine that was unlikely to give me food poisoning, and think on my feet when things would inevitably go wrong. Those skills would last my whole life and give me the confidence to take ambitious trips later in life. These days, I don't get stressed out when I need to plan a trip, and I am comfortable navigating foreign countries even when I don't know the language. But there are many other hobbies, such as playing guitar or photography, that feel as though they would be too time consuming and complicated for me to pick up now.

As we get older, it can seem daunting to learn the skills necessary to pursue a new hobby, just as it gets harder to switch to a job in a different industry. There's also some evidence that as we age, it is harder for us to learn new skills. Our brain structures change as we get older, making it more difficult for us to learn new behaviors. (This is something I explore further in the next chapter's section on habit formation.) But there are also practical concerns as you take on more responsibilities. These days, I can't just take up new leisure activities on a whim. I have to carefully count my vacation days and weekend hours and figure out how a hobby will fit into Ben's and Ella's schedules. Many hobbies also cost money; when you're younger, you have less money, but you also have more freedom to use it as you please. These days, with a mortgage and Ella's college fund to consider, I have to weigh the cost of a hobby within my family's budget.

If I had known that, I might have been more conscious about the hobbies I picked up in my twenties. In those years, what I did in my spare time was a little random. I flitted from poetry readings to drumming lessons to art-house films. I took an interest in my friends' hobbies too, trying them on for size. At one point, I knit the world's longest unfinished scarf because my friend Caitlin taught me the basics of knitting but never got around to showing me how to cast off. Kate once invited me to go snowshoeing near Lake Tahoe, but I was so much slower than everybody else in the party that I found myself utterly alone in the middle of a forest. All of that exploration was valuable and enriching, but in most cases, I did not invest enough time to become proficient at them. As a result, they never became hobbies and eventually faded out of my life. That's why there's a good chance that I'll never be a knitter or a snowshoer, unless I make a concerted effort to do those things now.

OUR LEISURE HOURS ARE SHRINKING

There's some evidence that today's twentysomethings might find it even harder to practice hobbies. The data show that for the first time in modern history, the amount of leisure time we have is actually shrinking rather than increasing. For decades, economists predicted that technology would increasingly shorten the workday and workweek, allowing workers to have far more free time to pursue hobbies and enjoy family life. But they were wrong; starting in the 1990s, people began working more, rather than less. That was particularly true for people with college degrees who were pursuing professional careers. It's worth taking a moment to see how we got here and why it might be worth fighting back against this trend.

For most of history, only the very wealthy had any free time at all; the rest of the population had to work when they could, tilling fields or tanning leather or whatever else they did to earn a living. Some historians believe that the idea that human beings could separate work hours from leisure hours first came about during the Industrial Revolution, when a person's time became a commodity that he or she could sell to an employer or withhold for themselves.[9]

But even a hundred years ago, factory workers often spent between ten and twelve hours on the job six days a week, which meant that their free hours were very limited. It was the privileged upper classes who developed the activities we now think of as classic hobbies, such as needlepoint, gardening, and stamp collecting. (This reminds me of my dear Miss Alice, whose ideas about hobbies seemed stuck in the Victorian age.) In fact, the economist Thorstein Veblen coined the term *leisure class* to refer to those who had the luxury to enjoy activities that required skills but were done for pleasure, rather than earning money.

Over the last century, things have changed. Time spent away from work is now considered a basic human right, partly because of all the medical data I referenced earlier that shows that leisure time makes people healthier and more psychologically sound. Throughout the twentieth century, the amount of leisure time steadily went up, thanks to improvements in technology that made both work and home chores less time consuming. Between 1965 and 2003, men gained 6.2 more leisure hours a week because they were spending less time working at their jobs. Women gained 4.9 extra leisure hours a week because they began spending more time in the corporate world and less time on housework and child care, resulting in a net gain in leisure time.[10] (But women still do more chores than men, which eats directly into their relaxation time. So guys: do us a solid and chip in with the laundry.)

According to the most recent data from the American Time Use Survey, a fascinating minute-by-minute accounting of the lives of thousands of people that the government has been conducting for decades, Americans spend five hours and thirteen minutes a day on leisure.[11] This includes time spent on both hobbies and socializing, which often overlap. Today, the average American has more than thirty-five hours of free time a week, or nearly two thousand hours a year. It may not feel like it, but it's true.

But here's where the story gets more complicated. Just because the sheer volume of free time in our lives has increased over the last hundred years, it doesn't mean that we are able to spend it cultivating hobbies. One study found that even as the quantity of leisure time has increased across the population, free time is often broken into smaller intervals, rather than enjoyed as a big chunk. This is particularly true of people who work in shifts, who must squeeze an hour of rest here or there in between work hours. And in dual-income families, women still do most of the household work and child care, which often means that their leisure time is more interrupted,[12] less relaxing, and generally less satisfying.[13]

What's more, research suggests that leisure time is effectively shrinking. Economists first spotted the trend in the early 1990s. They noticed that for the first time in history, highly educated people started spending more time working than their less educated counterparts.[14] (In other words, Veblen's notion of the "leisure class" no longer made sense.) And because more and more of the population is pursuing higher education and seeking professional careers, this means that as a society, we are actually moving in the direction of having less free time. Yikes!

Researchers are still trying to make sense of why this might be. For one thing, technology has not improved high-wage work as much as it has low-wage work. Automation and machinery have dramatically reduced the amount of human labor required in factory and agricultural work, for instance, compared to, say, law and medicine. But sociologists also point to a deeper shift surrounding the culture of work, particularly among people who have invested a lot of time and money in higher education, as we saw in the previous chapter. For a growing proportion of the population, work is an increasingly all-consuming endeavor, one deeply tied to identity and self-worth. Writing in *The Atlantic*, the journalist Derek Thompson said, "For the college-educated elite, [work] would morph into a kind of religion, promising identity, transcendence, and community."[15]

Today's twentysomethings are on track to have less time for hobbies than their parents and grandparents did. This is counterproductive. Research shows that leisure activities make us happier, healthier, and better able to cope with stress. All of this would improve our ability to tackle work-related challenges and curb our tendencies to overwork. But perhaps more important, it would allow us to find meaning and identity outside work, which is much better for our mental health.

HOW TO CULTIVATE YOUR PASSIONS
THROUGHOUT YOUR LIFE

How can we actually do this? How can we create space for hobbies throughout our lives? And how can we cultivate new ones? I am personally interested in these questions because I haven't been able to figure this out in my own life.

When I turned the corner of thirty, I found a job that I loved, and it was easy to throw myself into it. Then I gave birth to Ella, who took up what little free time I had with her gurgles and coos. My life is full of good things, but new hobbies aren't really part of the picture.

The truth is, I miss how colorful my life was back in my twenties, when I spent my leisure hours dipping my toes into different hobbies. Late one night in grad school, I was too tired to keep working on an essay, so I sauntered into my roommate Alan's room. I loved the song he was playing on his computer, which turned out to be by a band called Minus the Bear. We sat on the floor listening to every single one of their albums until the wee hours of the morning. For the next five years, Alan and I went to see Minus the Bear and other indie bands whenever they came to San Francisco. I loved every minute of it.

The hobbies I picked up in my twenties made me more curious about the world around me. And I learned about myself: what made me come alive, what made me happy, what sparked my creativity. I want to bring some of this back into my life. I've been searching for someone to show me how to do this—a person who has successfully managed to balance hobbies with other important life pursuits. And I think I've found the perfect guide. On a work trip to San Francisco, I met Stewart Thornhill, a fifty-five-year-old business school professor at the University of Michigan. Almost as soon as we started chatting, he shifted from talking about his job to talking about the rich life he has outside the office. I wanted to learn more.

Stewart says that he's tried to pick up a new hobby every ten years. It all began in his midtwenties, when he started learning various Japanese martial arts, working his way up to the very highest level of the practice. In his midthirties, he was keen for a new challenge, so he got a motorcycle and began riding across the country, sometimes with a crew of tough guys in leather jackets. In his forties, he started working toward a pilot's license. These days, he spends much of his free time in the sky.

I want to know how he's been able to pack so much into his life. His job keeps him busy with teaching, research, and administrative duties, and he's also a husband and a father. He makes it look easy, but as we sit down to breakfast, he makes it clear that it is not. He tells me that back in his twenties, when he discovered his passion for martial arts, he made a deliberate decision to make hobbies a central part of his life. He believes that the activities he does in his leisure hours are the key to staying emotionally balanced and intellectually curious in the midst of a busy, chaotic life. So he's made doing them a priority.

It hasn't always been easy. There have been times when he's felt as though there weren't enough hours in the day to churn out the vast quantities of research necessary to get to the next stage of his career. He often feels like the odd man out in a culture that prizes work above all else. "When I was doing martial arts, I had a class that met in the evening," he recalls. "I would often meet with students or colleagues after lecturing for the day, but at five, no matter what we were doing, I would pack up and leave. People would often give me a strange look, because this is just not what most professors do. But I had to stop caring what other people thought about me; I was fine being that weird guy who had a life outside of work."

Stewart has thought a great deal about why hobbies are important and how to incorporate them into your life. He gave me some useful advice.

Remember Why It's Worth It

In our culture, hobbies can sometimes feel like a luxury, something you get to do when you have checked the very last item off your "to-do" list. But Stewart says that if you want to incorporate hobbies into your life, you need to first believe that it is worth the time and effort. For him, hobbies are crucial to his happiness and sanity in academia, where it is common for professors to wrap their identity in the research they produce. Early in his career, Stewart watched as many of his colleagues were crushed when a research paper of theirs was rejected by a journal. Some would get depressed, fixate on what they could have done better, and question whether they should leave the field altogether.

Stewart wasn't immune to anxiety, but it was easier for him to put his work in perspective because he spent hours doing things unrelated to his day job. The people he meets through his hobbies aren't in academia, they don't care what he has, or hasn't, achieved at the office that day. At the dojo or on the road with a bunch of bikers, he sheds his identity as a professor. But perhaps more important, his hobbies allow him to stop thinking about his work. "I tend to pick hobbies that demand all of my attention in the moment," he says. "If you're not focused in martial arts, you'll get hit in the face. If you're not focused while on a motorbike or flying a plane, you could literally die. There's something meditative about training your mind to focus on what is directly in front of you instead of letting your thoughts wander."

You need to remember what value your hobby adds to your life. It might be about helping you relax and put your work in perspective. It might be about nurturing your curiosity about the world around you. Or it might be about giving yourself an opportunity to be creative. Knowing why you do a particular activity will enable you to keep at it even when you're crunched for time or when your colleagues give you the side-eye for taking off right at 5:00 p.m.

Pick a Hobby That Reflects Who You Are

Given how much time you will spend on your hobbies over the course of your life, Stewart says it is worth thinking carefully about what you select. You should pick activities that cultivate or express some part of yourself that does not come out at work or at home. It should also involve the right balance of challenging and familiar. For instance, Stewart realized that he enjoyed activities that allowed him to push his body to the limit. At the same time, he recognized that he was an introvert. He has settled on doing intense physical activities that allow him to spend time alone rather than, say, pursuing team sports. This has allowed his hobbies to be restorative, particularly after long days of having to interact with people.

Be Prepared for Challenges

After you commit to a hobby, Stewart says, it's important to be prepared for hurdles. One challenge is that it really does get harder to pick up new skills as the decades go by. Stewart takes joy in mastering each of his hobbies. But as he's gotten older, he's observed how much longer it takes to perfect each new skill. When he began taking flying lessons in his forties, he was often in classes with people half his age. "Their motor skills were just sharper than mine," he says. "I had to work harder and longer than they did to get as good. Part of the process of learning how to fly was about managing my own frustrations."

But there are payoffs to learning new skills as you get older. Neurologists have found that learning new skills can slow down age-related cognitive decline and stimulate new brain cell growth even into late adulthood. One study found that adults between sixty and ninety who learned a complex skill such as digital photography or quilting, which require good hand-eye coordination and rely on both short- and long-term memory, demonstrated major improvements in their overall memory three months later.[16] Pushing yourself to learn new skills throughout your life can help keep your mind nimble and sharp.

Stewart says that there will also be practical challenges. As he's gotten married and had a child, he's had to balance his hobbies with the needs of his family. Stewart's wife expressed worry about his safety on the road when he was on his motorbike after hearing about people getting into crashes, which was what convinced him to give it up. He moved on to flying, an activity that is dangerous but tends to have more security measures in place, which gives his wife some peace of mind. When Stewart's daughter was born, he realized that he no longer had time to do multiple hobbies, so he now limits himself to a single one. And as she gets older, Stewart is open to finding a new hobby based on her interests and passions, so they can do it together. "I've been flying for about ten years," he says. "So it's about time I picked up a new hobby anyway."

PRACTICE HOBBIES EARLY AND OFTEN

I was inspired by Stewart's story. The thing I took away from it was that hobbies don't just happen; they require planning and commitment. Stewart recognized the value of his hobbies in his twenties, and that allowed him to make space for them as his life filled up with other responsibilities in his thirties and beyond. If you're in the middle of your rocket years, you might take a page from Stewart's playbook. You can fill your leisure time with activities that tap into your interests and passions, then think about how to incorporate your favorite ones into your life going forward.

But perhaps, like me, you're past your twenties and have neglected this part of your life for a long time. It's never too late to rethink your leisure time. I began to see that if I wanted to have hobbies, I would have to carve out the time for them. It occurred to me that I often kept working on nights and weekends, but it wasn't because my editors expected me to; I did it because I enjoyed my job and wanted to be good at it. I decided that it wouldn't kill me to slow down a bit. So I tried something different for a change: I started clocking out after work and silencing my Slack alerts and emails. I suddenly found that I had some free time at my disposal. The question was: What would I do with it?

One evening, I was casually scrolling through my Instagram feed right after Ella had fallen asleep when one post stopped me in my tracks. With the dramatic words "Farewell" against a red background, Minus the Bear announced that it was retiring after seventeen years. I remembered how much fun I'd had going to concerts in my twenties and I wondered why I had stopped.

So twelve years after I first discovered Minus the Bear on the floor of Alan's room, I bought two tickets for their final tour. On a Thursday night in October, Ben and I got a sitter for Ella and took an Uber to the Paradise Rock Club in downtown Boston. We got a drink at the bar. And then the band came onstage and played songs that were familiar to me. I felt as I had years before, before we had a toddler sleeping soundly at home, before we had a mortgage, before we had careers that consumed so much of our time.

It was a powerful feeling. When neurologists do brain-imaging scans, they find that listening to the music of our youth enables us to tap into the emotions and experiences we had when we first listened to those songs, no matter how long ago that was. Our favorite songs function like a drug, stimulating the brain's pleasure circuit, releasing waves of feel-good neurotransmitters such as dopamine, serotonin, oxytocin.[17] The more we love a song, the more it becomes a kind of neurochemical narcotic.

That night, I was flooded with dopamine.

THREE

FITNESS

I arrive at the fitness studio ten minutes before class starts.

Before driving over, I spend an hour in front of the mirror figuring out what to wear. A week ago, I ordered four overpriced workout outfits online, and after trying them on one by one, I settled on fabulous red snakeskin leggings—complete with mesh cutouts at the thigh—and a matching top. It occurs to me, as I glance around at the other people stretching their backs and hamstrings before class, that I am a wee bit overdressed. Everybody else is in ratty old college T-shirts and shorts. I'm so out of place. But I shouldn't be surprised: I'm thirty-four, and this is the first time I'm working out in . . . well, really ever.

Researchers have found that there is a window in your late twenties when your exercise routines tend to be locked in for the rest of your life, impacting your lifelong health and longevity.[1] At the age of twenty-five, the patterns in your brain start becoming hardwired, resisting your efforts to create new ones. But the data show that people's activity levels decline in their rocket years, so most of us are locking in bad habits rather than good ones.[2] That certainly described me. A decade ago, I was subsisting on a diet of popcorn, ramen, and M&M's, while scrambling between job interviews, hot dates, and last-minute road trips. Working out was the last thing on my mind.

As I'm discovering right now, it *is* possible to pick up new habits later in life. It is just way harder. The reason I am here in the first place is that it has been a year since I gave birth to Ella, and I am still fifteen pounds over my prepregnancy weight. This has come as a bit of a shock to me, because through most of my twenties, my weight stayed squarely in the healthy BMI zone and did not seem to budge no matter how badly I neglected my health. My singularly sedentary lifestyle and terrible diet choices seemed to have no effect on my waistline. But as I entered my thirties, to my horror, all that began to change. These days, on a particularly indulgent vacation, I automatically go up a jean size. I begin to panic that I am losing control of my body. I have a recurring nightmare that I will get bigger and bigger, until one day I won't be able to leave my house and Ben will have to remove me by crane to take me out to dinner.

I may not be entirely wrong about my future if I don't stage an intervention—and soon. Weight loss researchers have found that our basal metabolic rate, the amount of energy it takes to keep our muscles, bones, and organs alive, begins to slow down at the age of twenty-five.[3] It keeps decreasing at a rate of 2 percent or more every decade for the rest of our lives.[4] In practice this means I am currently burning 50 to 100 fewer calories every single day now than a decade ago. Holly Lofton, the director of medical weight management at the New York University School of Medicine, says that most people don't start noticing how their bodies have changed until they are nearing thirty and their weight begins to creep up. Lofton says that the only way to fight back is to reduce our caloric intake or increase our physical activity. The reality begins to dawn on me: to avoid the crane-removal scenario, I may have to finally confront my fear of working out.

My terror of exercise can be traced back to middle school. It became pretty clear during my teenage years that I didn't have any coordination or athletic talent. I spent gym classes breathlessly running around a basketball court or soccer field, never actually making contact with the ball. I was never sure how I would be able to survive PE, so my brain was always shuffling through excuses to get out of it. (Can I deliberately sprain my ankle? How humiliating would it be to fake menstrual cramps?)

In eighth grade, I very nearly failed the national fitness test in Singapore, my sides aching after the mile-and-a-half practice runs. All of that came as a surprise to my father, who was a star athlete in his time. He excelled at every single sport presented to him: cricket, soccer, hockey, badminton, golf, even Ping-Pong. In most of the black-and-white photos I've seen of him as a boy, he is posing for team pictures, wearing shorts and smiling broadly. Often, he is the captain. He racked up so many trophies that his family didn't know where to put them. Trophy storage was not a particular problem I saddled on my family; instead, we huddled together at the dinner table, trying to figure out how I could pass the fitness test to avoid having to take remedial gym classes. My father very patiently took me to the park on weekends, helping me improve my running times just enough so that I could get a passing mark. He jogged beside me and walked with me when I couldn't run anymore.

All of this is to say that by the time exercise was no longer actually required by the education system, I felt a massive burden lifted from my shoulders. In my twenties, when spinning, barre, and Pilates classes became fashionable, I avoided them like the plague. When a new love interest asked me to go hiking or rock climbing on a date, I would politely decline and decide that a relationship with that individual would never work out.

So what the hell was I doing at this trendy workout studio in my snakeskin leggings? The truth is that it was an act of desperation. About a week before, I'd spent a miserable afternoon trying on every single dress in my closet to find something to wear to a cocktail party. Nothing had fit. In a moment of despair, I'd done a quick search for fitness studios close to my house. Orangetheory Fitness had popped up, promising a "total body transformation." I'd signed up on the spot.

So here I am. At 5:30 p.m., a muscular redhead bearing a remarkable resemblance to Johnny Bravo, complete with a curly lock of hair over his forehead, opens the door. He loudly announces that the class is starting, then proceeds to aggressively high-five everybody. Orangetheory's gimmick is making every member wear a monitor so we can watch our heart rates go up and down on a big screen. The idea is that if you keep your pulse in a high calorie-burning zone for most of the class, you will continue to burn more calories than normal for the next thirty-six hours.

My eyes glaze over as Johnny Bravo explains the workout, which involves rotating among weight training, rowing, and running. He gives me an enthusiastic thumbs-up. He never stops smiling. I decide to start the workout with running, since it is the only one of the three activities that I actually know how to do. I find an open treadmill and begin jogging at 2 miles an hour. My heart rate spikes up to the dangerous red zone. The dude next to me, who looks about sixty, is running at 7.5 miles an hour, not even breaking a sweat, and his heart rate still appears to be in a neutral blue zone.

"This is how I am going to die, isn't it?" I think. "I'll get a heart attack and roll off the treadmill, while Johnny Bravo over here blasts Van Halen in the background. He'll probably high-five the EMTs as they take away my body on a stretcher."

WHY IS EXERCISE SO IMPORTANT?

For me, showing up at the gym was a last-ditch effort to get my weight under control. After all, everyone from Oprah Winfrey to Gwyneth Paltrow says that exercise is the path to getting the trim, svelte body we all wish we had.[5] But what does science actually say about exercise and weight loss? As I dug into medical journals, I found that exercise can be very effective for keeping the pounds off, particularly as your metabolism slows down with age.[6] This was good news to me, because my weight had been slowly creeping up every year since I'd entered my thirties, and that was before the fifteen pounds I'd gained during pregnancy. However, research shows that in order to lose a significant amount of weight, exercise needs to be combined with calorie restriction.[7] So, in addition to schlepping to the gym, I would (ugh!) also have to cut down on my consumption of cake.

I admit that my eating habits had a lot of room for improvement. Throughout my rocket years, I was too busy to cook well-balanced meals. My diet consisted of a lot of takeout. I snacked a lot, particularly when I was stressed. (Chocolate and popcorn always do the trick for me.) I wasn't alone, apparently. A large-scale study found that people often pick up bad habits in the early part of their rocket years, when they start living by themselves: 60 percent of participants between the ages of eighteen and twenty-five did not eat enough fruits and vegetables, 39 percent did not eat three meals a day regularly, and 60 percent ate more than four unhealthy snacks a day, including chocolates, chips, and soda.[8] In my case, I had brought many of these bad eating habits with me out of my twenties and into my thirties. But since Ella had been born, I had been trying to change my ways and cook more nutritious meals, not just for my own sake but for hers.

The good news is that the combination of diet and exercise has been shown to lead reliably to weight loss. A longitudinal study from Brown University analyzing the habits of more than ten thousand adults who had lost at least thirty pounds and kept it off found that people who succeed in losing weight have a couple of things in common: They restrict their calorie intake, stay away from high-fat foods, and watch their portion size. But most important, they combine a good diet with regular exercise. In other words, exercise is a key to accelerating weight loss and keeping the weight off.[9]

As I explored the vast body of research about exercise, I found that weight loss is really just the tip of the iceberg when it comes to the benefits of exercise. Studies consistently find that people who work out regularly are able to prevent serious diseases, including many types of cancer, type 2 diabetes, high blood pressure, stroke, and Alzheimer's. But the one detail that really caught my attention is that regular exercise has been proven to extend a person's life by several years.

For decades, doctors assumed that exercise was good for longevity, but they did not have definitive proof. But in a landmark Harvard study from 1989, researchers found compelling evidence that having consistent fitness habits over the course of your life was directly tied to several extra years in your life span. The researchers tracked 16,939 members of the Harvard community between the ages of thirty-five and seventy-four over the course of twelve to sixteen years.[10] They looked back at participants' health records while they were in college, studying the results of their incoming freshmen physical exams. They noted whether each person was a varsity athlete, and if not, they asked about how much physical activity he or she did. After graduating, alumni were mailed surveys at regular intervals, asking about their current health and tracking any illnesses they developed. Finally, the researchers stayed abreast of death notices received by the Harvard alumni office and identified the cause of death of all participants who passed away. The scholars found that early death rates were lower among those who were more physically active. People who burned between 500 and 3,500 calories a week through exercise were less likely to die prematurely from heart and respiratory disease. By the age of eighty, the scholars could attribute up to two years of extra life to getting enough exercise rather than staying sedentary.

Until recently, that would not have been such a compelling detail to me. I didn't care much if I could tack on a few more geriatric years to my life. But that changed with Ella. Even though she is just a tiny thing right now, I often project forward to how old I will be when she's in college, when she gets married, or when she has a baby of her own. I would do anything for the chance to spend a few more healthy years with her in my old age. It turns out that exercise is a proven way to make that happen.

YOUR MIDTWENTIES FITNESS RESET BUTTON

In their study, the Harvard researchers uncovered an unexpected detail: as they analyzed the entire life cycle of the thousands of people in their study, they learned that how active you are as a child or a college student has no impact on adding additional years to your life. (This makes me feel a little better about faking illness in middle school gym classes.) In the study, they wrote that being very active in the first two decades of your life "carries little or no benefit in the later years." On the other hand, the exercise routines you form between the ages of twenty-five and thirty-five can be directly traced to a longer life span. In other words, establishing fitness habits in your rocket years is vital to setting you up for a long and healthy life.

The researchers found, for instance, that varsity athletes, many of whom had spent their childhoods playing sports, were no more likely to be healthier or live longer than people who had done no exercise in college. It was really their behaviors in the years after college that were predictive of how long they would live. If a varsity athlete stopped exercising in his post-college years, he would end up with the exact same mortality risk as alumni who had never exercised at all. On the flip side, participants who had not been particularly active in college but had developed good exercise routines in their postcollege years could gain additional years.

Another way to look at the findings is that people who happen to be genetically predisposed to being more athletic don't get a leg up when it comes to lifelong health and longevity. People like me who were the last ones picked for the dodgeball team still have a shot at being fit as adults. "Evidently, inheritance of a sturdy constitution (as implied by varsity athletic status) is less important to longevity than continuation of adequate life-time exercise," the researchers wrote.

All of that came as a surprise to me. I had assumed that my unfit childhood had already shaved years off my life. I had heard over and over that exercising as a child was the key to lifelong good health. That's what I had taken away from former first lady Michelle Obama's Let's Move! campaign, for instance. She went around the country getting children to be more active, Hula-Hooping with seven-year-olds one week and doing a workout routine with middle schoolers on *The Ellen DeGeneres Show* the next. As I studied the medical literature, I discovered that being fit as a child is certainly important because it can avert serious diseases such as childhood obesity and diabetes. But it is not predictive of a healthy adulthood or a longer life.

What this means is that all of us get a fitness reset button in our midtwenties. For those of us who spent our youths trying to sneak out of gym class, this is good news; as adults, we get another shot at creating healthy fitness habits that will carry us through our old age. On the other hand, people who were very sporty as kids need to make a deliberate choice to bring those fitness habits with them into their thirties and beyond. No matter where we start out on the fitness spectrum, our rocket years offer an opportunity to determine how healthy we will be throughout adulthood.

REALITY CHECK: IT'S REALLY HARD TO WORK OUT IN OUR ROCKET YEARS

Okay, it's time for a reality check. I am fully aware that it can be very hard to prioritize exercise in our twenties, even if we understand intellectually that fitness is important. After all, there are other big, equally important issues to worry about in our rocket years. Every few months, you're dealing with some sort of new existential dilemma: Why do people have children? Could this dude I just met on a Tinder date be my soul mate? And then there's the barrage of decisions you're dealing with on an everyday basis: Should I apply for this job? What should I wear to the job interview? Is it worth going on a second date with this person? All of these can derail your efforts to go to the gym.

Though I was a particularly inactive specimen of a twenty-something, the data show that most people become less and less fit as their twenties progress. Even people who loved exercise as children and college students can find it hard to keep working out regularly as they move through their rocket years. Researchers conducted a longitudinal study and found that people between the ages of eighteen and twenty-nine experienced "continuing erosion of activity patterns."[11] Women were more likely than men to see decreases in regular, vigorous activity, but the declines were consistent across both genders. Then, by the time people reached their thirties, their activity levels stayed fairly stable for the next three and a half decades.[12] If you're spending most of your time drinking beer on the couch at twenty-eight, there's a good chance you'll be doing so at sixty-eight, too. This supports the earlier Harvard study that showed that people's fitness habits between the ages of twenty-five and thirty-five have a great impact on their lives. All evidence suggests that by your early thirties, your exercise routines seem to be locked in for the rest of your life unless you consciously work to change them.

I saw that happen to my husband. Unlike me, Ben was an incredibly active kid. By high school standards, we lived in different galaxies: while I was preparing for speech competitions, Ben was at batting practice or fielding ground balls. When we met in college, he was the fittest I have ever seen him: he was always on the quad playing Frisbee or catching a pickup basketball games between classes. Yet throughout his rocket years, just as the data predict, his fitness levels plummeted. While he was working on his PhD, he struggled to find time to go for a run or join an intramural sports team. In more recent years, family obligations got in the way. These days, between a busy job and a child who consumes every last ounce of our attention, Ben seems to have decided that exercise is a lost cause.

But as someone who loved team sports growing up, Ben had a slightly different obstacle than I did: for him—and many other former athletes—exercise is not the same as sports. He was drawn to baseball because he loved the competition and bonding with his teammates. The fact that it also made him healthier was incidental. Yet most of the things that adults do to stay in shape are solitary activities such as running or lifting weights. Even group gym classes, like the one I'm doing, involve working out with complete strangers, then leaving in a hurry. None of this strikes Ben as appealing.

Shawn Sorenson, a health and exercise scientist at the University of Southern California, refers to someone like Ben as a "couch potato athlete." In a series of studies, he and his colleagues examined the fitness habits of five hundred students and alumni.[13] He discovered that former jocks were just as likely to end up becoming sedentary as people who had never done sports. In his interviews with those sporty types turned couch potatoes, he observed that today's athletes are coached in their sports from a very young age and follow carefully planned training regimens under constant guidance. If an athlete goes on to play in college, all of that training is taken up a notch: there is a whole network of coaches, physical therapists, dietitians, and sports psychologists supporting him or her. When these athletes graduate and are left to their own devices, many have trouble making the leap to doing exercise on their own. Sorenson thinks that it's hard for athletes who had so much external motivation to do sports—from their families, coaches, and teammates— to find the intrinsic motivation to do so.

And as I mentioned previously, having been fit as a kid or a college student has no impact on your health and life span unless you keep working out in your twenties and beyond. This also applies to high-performing athletes. A 2015 study tracking the life span of elite intercollegiate student athletes found that although those students were very fit during the time that they participated in the sport, the benefits of exercise did not last into later in life. "To realize life span health benefits," the study concluded, "it is imperative that student athletes maintain consistent patterns of healthy exercise beyond retirement from competitive sports."[14]

By the time Ben and I were in our late twenties, neither of us was in very good shape. It seemed odd to me that even though he had been a star athlete as a kid while I was always sitting on the bench during team sports, we had somehow ended up in the same place. Both of us were spending long hours at our jobs, eating out for most meals, and barely finding time to go on a leisurely walk on the weekend.

The scary reality is that it doesn't take long for unhealthy habits to affect us negatively. In 2017, the insurance company BlueCross BlueShield analyzed data from fifty-five million commercially insured people between the ages of twenty-one and thirty-six. It found that at the age of twenty-seven, many people's health began to decline.[15] The researchers said the drop-off was more than would be expected from normal aging. Those young people suddenly experienced higher-than-average levels of obesity, diabetes, and depression, as well as endocrine and cardiovascular disease. It's terrifying to think that those data might be describing you or me!

Most people aren't fully aware of how easy it is to slide into inactivity in their twenties. It tends to happen so imperceptibly that most of us don't see it happening. You get pulled into an exciting project at the office, which has you working long hours, so you skip your evening run. You move to a new city and never get around to signing up at a gym. You fall in love and want to spend every spare moment with your significant other, which means sacrificing your Saturday-morning basketball game.

But knowledge is power. If you're armed with data showing that the most common pattern of behavior is to become less active in your rocket years, you can be more alert to your own routines. You can observe when you might be slipping into a sedentary lifestyle. You can make an extra effort to create fitness habits and stick to them. And if you're like me and miss the window to get fit in your rocket years, it's never too late to get started. (Though, as you're about to see, it might take more willpower.)

HABIT FORMATION GETS HARDER AS WE GET OLDER

How exactly can you act on all of this knowledge? How can you take all your good intentions and turn them into an exercise habit?

There's actually a lot of research that can help with this. For more than a decade, neuroscientists have been fascinated with the science of habit formation. Using scanners and sensors to study our brain activity, they have found that learning a new behavior and turning it into a habit is a complex neurological process that involves making connections among many parts of the cerebral cortex. They've also found that we can hack our brains to create new habits by giving ourselves the right cues and rewards.

First things first. Neurologists have found that the younger we are when we create a new habit, the easier it will be. From the time we are born until the age of about twenty-five, our brains are still forming, which makes it easier to pick up new concepts and behaviors.[16] When we learn something new, we form links between different parts of our brains, or what neurologists call "neural pathways." To take a simple example, when you see a new word, some neurons in your visual cortex register the spelling of the word, others in your auditory cortex recognize its pronunciation, while still others in the associative region of your brain relate the new word to your existing knowledge.[17] When we are young, our brains have more plasticity to create these neural networks, which is why children are able to learn new languages so easily.

But this begins to change in our midtwenties.[18] The more we use the same neural pathways over and over, the more they move into deeper portions of our brain. In other words, they begin to become hardwired. Our brains are inclined to revert back to existing neural pathways rather than going through the effort of creating new ones. Or, in the words of MIT neuroscientist Tara Swart, our brains are "inherently lazy" and will choose the most energy-efficient path if left to their own devices.[19] And since creating habits is inherently a learning process, it is much harder to create new habits as we get older.

But apart from neurology, there are other reasons our twenties are an important time to establish healthy habits. For most of us, it is the first time we have control over our lifestyle. Until our rocket years, other people shape many of our everyday routines. When we are children, our parents set our bedtimes; coaches make us show up for sports practice and workouts. In college, we eat our meals in the dining hall. But suddenly, in our early twenties, we're spun out into the world, living on our own. We get to choose when we go to sleep and wake up. We must figure out what to eat at mealtimes. And we must decide if and when we're going to squeeze a workout into our packed schedules. In the words of Charles Duhigg, who wrote *The Power of*

Habit: Why We Do What We Do in Life and Business, all of our habits are "up for grabs" in our twenties.[20]

There were many reasons why it would have been much easier for me to create a workout routine in my twenties. Now that I'm in my thirties, not only am I faced with creating new habits from scratch, I must also fight back against many habits in my life that were ingrained over the last decade. But by the same count, if I don't get serious about fitness now, it is only going to get harder in my forties and fifties.

THE THREE-PART HABIT LOOP

In the end, I did survive my first Orangetheory workout—but just barely. After my close brush with death on the treadmill, Johnny Bravo made the class do sumo squats while holding a barbell, which seemed to be some kind of medieval torture. The next day, my thighs were screaming in agony. The act of sitting down was almost more than I could bear, so I spent the day in bed, taking ibuprofen every six hours.

I had absolutely no desire to drag myself back for a second class. In my head, I knew that working out is important; I had read all the studies. But each time I pulled up my Orangetheory app to book my next workout, I kept coming up with reasons not to go through with it. Maybe I could go tomorrow? Sleep is important, too! I should probably just sleep in. Don't I have a big work deadline coming up? On top of this barrage of excuses, I already had a daily routine that felt hard to change: I woke up, got Ella ready for school, worked all day, then made dinner. Adding an hour-long workout to the mix should not have been such a big deal, but when I was confronted with doing it, it felt like a gargantuan effort.

I wasn't just imagining it; creating new habits can be very hard, for all the neurological reasons I listed above, and in practice, your brain's resistance often comes in a stream of justifications and excuses. According to Duhigg, who spent years studying the neurology of habit, our brains are designed to stay on autopilot as much as possible, which allows us not to have to make so many decisions. Our habits allow us to avoid thinking about the behaviors that fill our days: waking up, showering, brushing our teeth, fastening our seat belt, starting the car. If we had to think through each of these steps, we would get overwhelmed and not be able to focus on higher-level cognitive functions, such as solving hard problems at work. Our brains actively resist changes to our habits and routines. So if it felt as though my brain was sabotaging my good intentions to work out, that's because it was.

So how does anybody create a new habit? What could I do to not only go back to the gym a second time but actually make it a habitual behavior that I would do without thinking? Duhigg says that neurologists have found that every habit has three components: a cue that triggers the behavior to start, the behavior itself, and then a reward. The last step, the reward, is a crucial part of habit formation at the start, but over time, as the behavior becomes more automatic, it becomes less important.

As a simple example, consider how monkeys can be trained to learn a new habit. In one experiment, neuroscientists placed monkeys in front of a computer monitor. A color would flash on the screen, and if they pushed the button with the corresponding color on it, they would get a drop of blackberry juice, which they love. But over time, pressing the color buttons became a habitual behavior. They would do it even without the yummy juice treat. And when the scientists studied the monkeys' brains, they found that the neural pathway dictating the button pressing had become thicker and thicker.

Duhigg says that similar patterns govern the way that humans create habits. By creating a cue-and-reward system, we can trick our brains into doing a particular behavior that, over time, can become so habitual that the reward is unnecessary. Many studies show that this strategy works very well in the context of creating fitness routines.

Duhigg cites a 2002 study from New Mexico State University in which researchers studied how people create exercise habits. They looked at 266 people who worked out at least three times a week. Most of the subjects had started exercising almost on a whim—much like I did. In some cases, they'd simply had some free time or needed an outlet for stress. But the reason that some people stuck to the habit while others didn't was that they identified a specific cue and a specific reward. Both had to be present in order for the behavior to become automatic. The cue could involve anything from lacing up their shoes before breakfast or winding down work to get ready for a 5:00 p.m. run. The reward could be anything that the subject truly enjoyed, from the feeling of accomplishment from logging the number of miles to eating dessert at dinner after a workout.

When it comes to fitness, Duhigg says, the rewards that are inherent in exercise, such as the endorphin rush after a long run, are not enough to motivate most people to keep working out. So at the start, it helps to create a reward for yourself after exercising, such as a small piece of chocolate. "This is counterintuitive, because most people start exercising to lose weight," Duhigg wrote in a *New York Times* article. "But the goal here is to train your brain to associate a certain cue ('It's 5 o'clock') with a routine ('Three miles down!') and a reward ('Chocolate!')." Eventually, he says, the behavior will become so ingrained that, like those monkeys, you won't need the treat anymore.[21]

All of this sounds very intriguing to me. Rather than just trying to drag myself to the gym because it is good for me (so I don't, you know, get sick and die prematurely), I decide to give myself a more immediate and exciting reward. Ordinarily, the chocolate idea would have been very appealing to me, but I was trying to decrease my overall calorie intake to help with my weight loss efforts. So I chose to reward myself with something else that I love: clothes. After every Orangetheory session, I would buy myself a new article of workout clothing. That made sense, since I hadn't had a single workout outfit until I got the red snakeskin one that I wore to my first workout. Over the next few weeks, I would show up in the most remarkable (okay, maybe a little ridiculous) gym clothes for each workout, from metallic blue getups to black leatherlike pants to tops that have to be tied in complex ways. I tried not to care that I was obviously the only one at the gym who cared even remotely about fashion.

The strategy seemed to work, though it was by no means easy. For the first couple of weeks, I kept talking myself out of working out. I noticed that going to the gym was eating into my leisure hours: I had less time to read in the afternoon or look through recipes to decide what to cook for dinner. But despite all of that resistance, I managed to drag myself to the 5:30 p.m. class three times a week. When I got back, I would reward myself by picking out cute new leggings or socks or tank tops online. After about a month, the routine started to set in. At 5:00 p.m. on Mondays, Wednesdays, and Fridays, I would automatically put on my gym clothes and head out the door. The prospect of picking out a new outfit stopped being such a big motivator, partly because at that point I had a fully stocked drawer of workout clothes. So I eventually stopped shopping for new clothes after class.

Duhigg says that not all habits are created equal. Researchers have found that there are some habits, which Duhigg calls "keystone habits," that have the power to kick-start a chain reaction that changes other habits in their wake. Exercise is one of them. People who successfully create a fitness routine often start eating better, too. "When you learn how to change your life through exercise, something that seems so hard and scary before . . . you start reanalyzing how much control you have over everything," Duhigg says.[22] That happened to me. Even before I started working out, I had been trying to cook more and prepare more nutritious food for my family. But going to the gym regularly convinced me that profound change was possible. I found that I had more willpower to say no to popcorn at the movies and swap the pasta dinners for grilled salmon and veggies.

A year later, I am still going to the gym regularly. I'm a smidge away from my prepregnancy weight, but perhaps more important, I feel stronger than ever before. As I kept going back week after week, I found that I could run longer distances at higher speeds. I found myself grabbing heavier weights. I began to notice how it was affecting my everyday life. It became easier to pick Ella up and carry her around. When I had to run through an airport to catch a flight, I wasn't out of breath when I got to the gate.

That was a revelation to me. My entire life, I had imagined myself to be the least athletic person to walk the planet, with no agility or muscular strength to speak of. Yet here I am, a regular gym rat. It's forcing me to rethink everything I know about myself. I wish I had started working out a decade ago, before my metabolism took a nosedive and so many of my adult routines became entrenched. But I'm proof that it's never too late to start exercising, even after years—or in my case, a lifetime—of inactivity. And the benefits of these workouts could stretch on for decades, keeping me strong and healthy as I get older.

To me, the most shocking thing of all is that I am kind of enjoying the workouts. I'm no longer getting flashbacks to dodgeball in middle school. In fact, I look forward to that one moment in every class when I'm running at my fastest speed on the treadmill with techno beats blasting overhead. Johnny Bravo has carefully timed the music to the pace of my run. I feel my body flooded with endorphins. On the way out, Johnny stands by the door, holding his muscular bicep out to enthusi-astically high-five me. Breathless and drenched in sweat, I slap his palm with every last ounce of strength left in my body.

FOUR

MARRIAGE

Ben and I are sitting in a private dining room at India Palace. Every single piece of furniture is covered in red velvet fabric. Enormous gold elephant statues nestle in corners. Someone has decided to pipe Bollywood's greatest hits through the sound system. It's all very festive, but the ambience feels like overkill because we are the only two people here, perched on chairs that appear to be modeled after the coronation thrones of eighteenth-century Mughal emperors. If I had known about all this fanfare, I would maybe not have come in sweatpants.

On the other hand, the elasticized waistband on my velour trousers comes in handy because on the long table in front of us, there is more food than I have ever seen in my life. There are mountains of samosas and pakoras and chutneys. Four servers in large turbans have laid out nine silver platters, and it's clear from their expectant faces that our job is to sample every single dish. "Do you think they got confused?" I whisper to Ben after they file out of the room. "Maybe they think this *is* the wedding?"

Nope. India Palace was aware that this was just a tasting session. We were the ones who were confused; we hadn't understood that when you tell a restaurant you're considering bringing it on as your wedding caterer, it will ply you with ungodly quantities of food, so you'd better come prepared with an empty stomach. Ordinarily, Ben and I would have been totally down with getting bribed with tandoori chicken and naan, but this was the fourth tasting we had attended in as many days. The night before, we had chowed down on barbecued spare ribs with grits and collard greens. The night before that, we had devoured filet mignon, roast duck, and baked salmon. I was pretty sure that one of us was going to die of a heart attack before we could say our vows.

At twenty-nine, exactly a decade after Ben and I had met as college freshmen, we got engaged. We decided to have the wedding in Atlanta, his hometown, and had flown down for a week to sort out the logistics. When caterers and wedding planners heard that we were college sweethearts, they waxed lyrical about how lucky we were to have found our soul mates so early in life. I didn't want to ruin the mood by telling them that, actually, the last ten years hadn't been a walk in the park. They'd been tempestuous, full of tears, shouting matches, and therapy. It turns out that figuring out if someone is the love of your life can be very stressful.

It started out as a by-the-book college romance. I saw Ben at a basketball game and thought he was cute. Having learned from *Sex and the City* that I couldn't wait around for a man to ask me out, I found Ben later that evening, gave him my phone number, and asked him to call me. To my surprise, he did. We went to a bar, then, a few days later, got coffee at the Hungarian Pastry Shop, and then went for a long walk in Central Park.

(Cue the romantic comedy montage.) After that, we were inseparable. We read on the lawn and made out in the stacks. We had loud quarrels on the quad about things that only college students argue about: How can I date someone who doesn't go to political protests? How compatible can we really be if you don't like the Beatles?

But once we graduated, the cracks in our relationship began to show. Every time we tried to talk about the future, it ended in an ugly fight. The underlying problem was that neither of us knew how to handle the issue of marriage. Did we want to get married at all? And to each other? And if so, when? In our midtwenties, we felt ill equipped to answer those questions, so instead, we sniped at each other. Months went by when we were more unhappy than happy. One day, while waiting at a stop sign, we decided to call it quits right there in the car. A few months later, Ben had flown to the other side of the country. We were twenty-five and single.

You know how the story ends. Ben and I eventually clawed our way back into each other's lives. In our three years apart, we sorted out our careers and dated other people, which gave us new clarity. I missed Ben's kindness and intelligence, but mostly I missed being with someone who really seemed to get me. That spark of mutual understanding is what many people mean when they talk about finding the love of their life. It turned out that Ben had been mine all along. At twenty-eight, after yet another failed relationship—this time with a volatile British sculptor—I gave Ben a call. He picked up. He wasn't dating anyone at the time and wanted to reconnect. Days later, he flew to see me in California, and months after that, we were engaged.

Getting married at the tail end of our rocket years was a classic millennial move. Today, half of all American adults[1]— and 65 percent of those with college degrees[2]—are married.

Among millennials who aren't married, 70 percent hope to be.[3] But Americans are delaying this milestone later than ever. On average, women marry at age twenty-eight, and men marry at thirty.[4] Couples tend to date for a long time—around six and a half years—before tying the knot.[5] In other words, dating and pondering marriage tend to occupy a lot of people's attention in their twenties.

THE GOLDEN AGE OF SOUL MATES

The idea of searching for, and marrying, someone you love seems like an obvious idea in our time. But it's actually a very new notion. "For most of history, it was inconceivable that people would choose their mates on the basis of something as fragile and irrational as love," wrote the historian Stephanie Coontz in *Marriage, A History: How Love Conquered Marriage.*[6]

Instead, marriage was a practical arrangement that ensured people's financial stability and position within the social order. The average person had little choice when it came to selecting a spouse. If the union wasn't arranged by his or her family, he or she would select from a few options based on whether a potential spouse was from the right family or could afford to pay a dowry. Coontz says that there is evidence that many married couples in history loved each other, but often, it grew out of years of living, working, and raising a family together. "Love was a bonus, not a necessity," she wrote.[7]

The idea of marrying for love has taken root only in the last two hundred years. But even over the last few decades, it was more a lofty ideal than an everyday reality. Until women had financial independence, marriage would never be just about companionship but about finding someone to support them.

For some, love was not a consideration at all. One study from 1967 found that 76 percent of women would be willing to marry someone they didn't love, as long as he could support a family.[8]

For millennials and Gen Zers, everything is different. Social conventions have drastically changed. It is far more acceptable to have sex and children outside of marriage. Matrimony is no longer seen as a rite of passage to adulthood. Today, women make up 47 percent of the workforce,[9] and more women than men graduate from college (34 percent versus 26 percent).[10] This means that women don't need to depend on their husbands for financial security and are freer to marry for love. We can pick a spouse based on sexual attraction, emotional connection, and shared values.

The good news is that most of us do find the right person. The vast majority of married Americans—88 percent—say they wed their best friend. And about 60 percent of them say they are extremely satisfied with their relationship.[11] Millennials and Gen Z couples have an even higher rate of relationship satisfaction at 65 percent. We're incredibly lucky. We are among the first generations of people in history who can marry someone we don't just love but also *like*.

The current approach to marriage appears to be working well. The divorce rate is at a forty-year low, with only sixteen divorces for every one thousand marriages. Millennials are driving the trend: over the last ten years, the divorce rate has declined by 18 percent, and predictions suggest it will continue to decline for years to come.[12] Sociologists believe that millennials are positioned to weather the storms of marriage in part because this generation waits longer to tie the knot, giving them more time to find the right partner and develop maturity and financial stability. This is encouraging news! If you're on a quest to find the love of your life, your chance of succeeding couldn't be better.

WHY WE GET MARRIED

Today we can marry by choice rather than from necessity. As a result, more people skip marriage altogether. Back in the 1960s, nearly 90 percent of Americans over the age of eighteen married, but today that figure hovers at about 50 percent.[13] The share of Americans who have never married is at a historic high of 20 percent.[14] But don't let this alarm you; many of these people have happy long-term relationships and even live with their partners, so they are just choosing to skip the marriage paperwork. Today, 9.4 percent of people between eighteen and twenty-four live unmarried with their partners, and among those twenty-five to thirty-four, that goes up to 14.8 percent.[15]

So what compels people to marry today? Our reasons for tying the knot are deeply personal and span the gamut. Some of us practice a religion that values marriage, while others might be in it for the more favorable tax bracket. Overwhelmingly, though, we marry because we're in love. The vast majority of Americans—88 percent—say that the most important reason to get married is love, followed by making a lifelong commitment (81 percent) and enjoying companionship (76 percent).[16] When it comes down to it, Americans are still a very romantic bunch.

Marriage offers other practical advantages that influence people's thinking. About half of Americans believe that having children is an important reason to get married,[17] and research makes a convincing case that marriage helps create conditions for parents to raise children effectively. While the child poverty rate among married households is 11 percent, that shoots up to 47 percent for children in opposite-sex cohabiting households and 48 percent in single-mother households.[18] Children of unmarried parents suffer from depression and drop out of school at higher rates, too.[19] (Keep in mind, though, that statistics like these don't reflect the fact that people who decide to marry have more resources in the first place, which complicates any simple comparison of outcomes for children in married versus unmarried households.)

Even so, marriage clearly does *cause* some differences in the context in which children are raised. For example, married couples can take advantage of economies of scale: they share expenses and pool their funds to invest in assets such as houses and cars. Due in part to factors like these and in part to who decides to marry in the first place, married people tend to have more money than single folks. In fact, 28 percent of people say that financial benefits are a good reason to get married.[20]

According to the Census Bureau, the 2010 net worth of a married couple between the ages of fifty-five and sixty-four averaged $261,405.[21] On the other hand, a single man of the same age averaged $71,428 and a single woman had $39,043. I found it extremely annoying and retrograde when my nosy aunties in Singapore kept telling me to get married to make sure I was financially secure. What century are we in? Had they not even heard about feminism? As much as I hate to admit it, though, part of their anxieties about my financial future may have been grounded in fact. (But still, aunties, stop telling your nieces and nephews what to do in their love lives! Just stay out of it!)

Finally, marriage appears to be good for your health.[22] Compared to single people, married folks live longer and have lower rates of depression. They have fewer strokes and heart attacks. They are less likely to have advanced cancer at the time of diagnosis and are more likely to survive cancer longer.[23] Doctors believe that there are several reasons for these outcomes. Some of this simply has to do with the fact that close relationships of all kinds—including friendships, as we'll see later in the book—lead to better health. The other reason is that having a spouse encourages people to take better care of themselves. Married people tend to take fewer risks, eat better, and go to the doctor more frequently.[24] Case in point: I recently asked Ben to go to the doctor to check out a new freckle that had appeared on his back. He dragged himself to the clinic to appease me, and it turned out to be nothing. But the research suggests that spousal nagging is entirely justified!

If you're considering marriage, these additional benefits of marriage will be peripheral rather than central to your thinking. But knowing how marriage could affect your life in the years to come is valuable knowledge, especially if you're contemplating whether to make your love official. And if you decide you're not the marrying kind, understanding these trends can help you take measures to ensure that you have the best quality of life. This might mean staying on top of your finances, paying extra attention to how your child is doing in school, and making sure you go for your medical checkups.

HOW CAN YOU TELL IF YOU'VE FOUND THE ONE?

The data show that most people want to get married. Half of Americans are married, and half of the never-married crowd hopes to tie the knot at some point.[25] But in some ways, finding a partner is more complicated for our generation than it was in the past. Figuring out if someone will be a good breadwinner is far more straightforward than figuring out if your partner is, you know, the one true love of your life.

Falling in love is a subjective experience, but researchers have some ideas about what brings two people together in the modern world. One clue can be found in the concept of the "soul mate," which two-thirds of Americans say they believe in.[26] This is an ancient notion with roots in many cultures. In the Greek text *The Symposium*, for instance, Plato talked about how humans originally had four arms, four legs, and a single head made of two faces. Zeus, the most powerful god, split the creatures in half, leaving every person wandering through life searching for his or her other half. Stories like this still have a powerful pull on our imagination, shaping what we're looking for in a partner.

When people talk about soul mates, researchers have found, they really tend to mean someone who understands them, often because they come from a similar background and see the world in a similar same way. (Unlike the ancients, who believed in one single soul mate for each person, today most of us believe there could be many partners out there with whom we could share this special bond.) Sixty-one percent of Americans say that partners should be similar to each other.[27] A smaller minority believe that couples should have a combination of similarities and differences. To put it another way, most of us are looking for a romantic partner who feels familiar, even if we've just met him or her. We are looking for someone who instinctively gets us and shares our worldview.

But what does "similar" really mean? After all, there are so many ways to identify commonalities with another person. There are socioeconomic factors, such as whether someone grew up in a middle-class or working-class family. There are ways of seeing the world, including religious and political points of view. And then there are personality traits, such as whether you're introverted or extroverted.

Social scientists have studied all of these dimensions of similarity in relationships and have found that *all* of them are relevant in marriage. For a long time, researchers have observed that people tend to marry people like themselves. The scientific term for this is *assortative mating*. This concept applies to the animal kingdom, too, so for all of our sophisticated notions about love, our mating behavior is more similar to that of monkeys and ladybugs than you might think. And in our current culture, where more people than ever marry for companionship, this trend has grown even more common. Studies find that people are more likely to fall in love with and marry people who share their class background, values, and personality. What's more, the more similar people are on all these fronts, the happier their marriages tend to be.

One recent study found that newlyweds tended to share religious and political beliefs.[28] Another found that they tended to share similar levels of charitable giving.[29] (This makes sense: you'd be pretty annoyed if your spouse gave away all your money to save the whales when what you really wanted was to make a down payment on a house.) And, among millennials and Gen Zers, the most common example of assortative mating is that people pair up based on educational backgrounds and earning potential. This is a relatively new phenomenon. Until the 1980s, couples rarely had the same level of education because most women did not attend college. But members of our generation can pick spouses who are similarly educated to themselves.

Why do these pairings happen? For one thing, the years in which we pursue higher education overlap with the years we're searching for life partners. Facebook's data scientists have found that 28 percent of married college graduates on the platform attended the same college.[30] Then, in your postcollege years, you're likely to end up in workplaces or social circles with people who share your educational background. It's also true that people tend to search out people who have similar educations. On dating apps, for instance, users commonly filter out people less educated than they are.[31]

It turns out that marrying someone like you is a pretty good strategy for marital happiness.[32] Psychologists think that people with similar educational and socioeconomic backgrounds tend to gravitate toward each other because these life experiences play a big role in shaping their identity and outlook. Two people who grew up in middle-class households likely share ideas about the value of money or the ideal division of labor at home. Having similar points of view about core issues—including children, money, religion, and politics—tends to minimize marital conflict.[33] Of course, all couples will have areas of difference. (That's partly what makes relationships interesting!) But conflicts over these bigger issues tend to be more lethal to a marriage than fights over personal preferences such as where to go on vacation or what to do on date night. Take this from Ben and me, who have never once agreed on what movie to watch, *ever*.

Studies show that couples tend to pick a partner with a similar personality, and the more similar they are, the happier they tend to be.[34] This refers to qualities that are partially innate, including things such as how open you are to new experiences, how easygoing you are, and how outgoing you are in social settings. One study found that personality traits seemed to matter more later in a marriage than in the early stages. In other words, people tended to connect over similar values, and over time, in day-to-day married life, how well a couple got along depended on how well they negotiated character differences.

One important takeaway from all this research is that you're more likely to find marital bliss with someone who shares your fundamental values and vision of family life. The thing is, it can take time to figure these things out for yourself because this self-knowledge comes slowly, with time and experience. This doesn't mean you need to figure everything out before you start dating. Instead, you should see what you learn about yourself from each new relationship. It will become clear to you whether you want children, how demanding your career will be, and whether religion is important to you. As you figure out what matters to you and what you want from life, pause and take stock. This information will help you decide whether to get more serious with a partner or even marry him or her. And remember, you and your partner are never going to be on the same page on every single issue. But identifying possible areas of conflict will allow you to talk things through. Together, you can decide whether a difference is a deal breaker or just something you'll have to work on in your relationship.

THE MARVELOUS MATCHMAKING INTERNET

Our generation believes in marrying soul mates, and we've come up with online dating technologies that help us geolocate them, wherever they might be in the world. These platforms make it easy to search for people based on preferences about age, looks, or education levels. Then the system learns from our behavior—the profiles we click on, the people we swipe right on—to keep feeding us more matches we'll like. The internet is now the most effective matchmaker in the United States: 39 percent of heterosexual couples and 60 percent of same-sex couples met online in 2017.[35] And although the media sometimes paint a picture of twentysomethings turning to dating apps mainly to hook up, the data tell a different story. A recent study found that 63 percent of millennials and 70 percent of Gen Zers are looking for a serious relationship when they open an online dating app.[36]

The origins of online dating go back to the early days of the internet. In 1995, Internet Explorer launched, and the same year, the online dating service Match.com went live. Soon the internet was flooded with dating platforms of all kinds, from Jdate to eHarmony to OKCupid to Grindr to Tinder to Bumble. For a long time, online dating carried a stigma. Many people felt it signaled that they weren't desirable enough to meet their partner through traditional venues, such as a school or bar. But for Gen Zers and millennials, dating apps are not just the norm; they're the number one way American couples meet each other. They're particularly helpful for people who have a smaller pool of possible partners, including people in small towns, older straight people, and, most dramatically, the LBGTQ community.

Online dating has made it harder, though, for people to form romantic connections offline.[37] You're less likely to find the love of your life by chatting someone up in the grocery line or coffee shop. In the past, couples would meet through friends, coworkers, and family or in places such as high school, college, or church. Over the last twelve years, there's been a steep decline in couples meeting in all these places. Your friends now have less reason to set you up on a blind date because your smartphone will do it more efficiently. If Ben and I were in college now, all signs suggest that he might turn me down if I hit on him after a basketball game; instead, he'd pick up his smartphone to find a date on Tinder or Match.com.

When online dating was relatively new, social scientists wondered whether offering users millions of possible options might allow them to meet, date, and fall in love with people from different backgrounds whom they would never meet in their school or neighborhood.[38] But when presented with infinite options, online daters seek out people similar to themselves along many dimensions, including education,[39] race,[40] religion,[41] and political ideology.[42] As we have seen, this pattern mimics how people select partners offline.[43] The internet just makes it easier to find people like yourself by letting you explicitly state your preferences, then searching the vast set of possible matches.

Online daters also like to throw a couple of "aspirational" candidates into the mix, according to researchers. For heterosexual couples, this usually involves men picking women who are younger and more attractive than they are and women picking older and wealthier men. Yeah, I know, what a shocker! It turns out that we can actually be very shallow when it comes to whom we date. "[Users] are aware of their position in the hierarchy and adjust their behavior accordingly, while, at the same time, competing modestly for more desirable mates," one study reads.[44] I wish aspirational daters good luck! But I also ask them to remember that people whose dating profiles generate a lot of interest tend to pair up with partners with similar levels of desirability. It's just the way of the world.

Still, the research about online dating represents, overall, good news. The internet has made it easier than ever to find your ideal partner. If there's a problem with online dating, it's perhaps that it works a little too well. Some online daters say they feel overwhelmed by the number of matches they receive on these platforms. In *Modern Romance: An Investigation*, Aziz Ansari interviewed online daters. Many said they were drowning in too many choices. Many users—women more than men—felt flooded with so many requests that they experienced decision paralysis and couldn't figure out who to move forward with.

Ansari also found that when online daters actually went on dates, their standards were often so high that they were willing to give up very good matches in the hope that an even better one was just around the corner. As a result, they exhausted themselves by going on date after date without ever feeling chemistry with any of their dates. The solution, he said, is to slow down a bit. "In most cases, people's unique traits and values are difficult to recognize, let alone appreciate, in an initial encounter," he wrote. "People's deeper and more distinctive traits emerge gradually through shared experiences and intimate encounters, the kinds we sometimes have when we give relationships a chance to develop but not when we serially first date."[45]

Technology can take the humanity out of the dating process and make people seem interchangeable, ultimately lowering your chances of creating a real connection. If you've bothered to go on a date with someone, take the time to get to know him or her. And if the date went fairly well—even if it wasn't perfect— perhaps give the person another chance?

Or try doing what my friend Matt does: when he's gone on a couple of dates with someone and things are going well, he suggests spending a month dating each other exclusively, to give the relationship a chance to blossom. At the end of that period, the two of them reevaluate the relationship. In a few cases, either Matt or his date decided that they shouldn't proceed. But in the end, he eventually found his now-fiancé. By giving his partners an off-ramp partway through the relationship, he increased the chances that the relationships he did pursue were with people who also chose to invest a lot in the relationship.

IS THERE AN IDEAL TIME TO GET MARRIED?

When I turned the corner on twenty-seven, something weird happened. After years of receiving nothing but flyers and bills in my mailbox, my postman began delivering something else: colorful invitations printed on thick card stock for my friends' engagement parties, wedding showers, and receptions. It blindsided me. For years, marriage hadn't seemed to be on anybody's agenda. My Facebook feed had been full of people celebrating new jobs and promotions, but then overnight, it was all diamond rings and six-tier cakes. At the time, I had been single for a few years, and my first thought was: Oh, God! I need to find myself a spouse ASAP! Maybe this guy next to me at Starbucks is single?

Looking back, the timing made sense. Throughout our twenties, my friends and I had been squeezing dates between our other pursuits. Along the way, some of us had gotten more serious with our partners. Often, those couples would move in together. As we saw earlier, the rate of cohabitation has been on the rise for decades.[46] The thing that seemed to nudge people toward marriage was starting a family. These days, college-educated women have their first baby at the age of 30.3 years on average.[47] And as we've seen, the vast majority of those women will get married before starting a family.

All of this raises the question: Is there an optimal time to get married? The short answer is yes. Economists have crunched the numbers and found that couples who get married between the ages of twenty-eight and thirty-two are least likely to get divorced later.[48] I know that this information can be terrifying, but please don't panic, drop this book, and get married this afternoon, like I wanted to do! The researchers used data on an enormous number of people, with varied experiences and characteristics, which means that plenty of couples who married before or after that window also stayed happily married. It's more valuable to understand the trends and behaviors underlying those numbers.

For a long time, social scientists believed that couples who married older tended to have more stable, long-lasting marriages. The conventional wisdom was that marriage is a difficult relationship, so marrying later enables you to know yourself better and find a compatible spouse. It also allows you to develop the maturity to tackle the challenges of married life. But a few years ago, the sociologist Nicholas Wolfinger spotted an interesting trend: when he studied a decade's worth of data from the National Survey of Family Growth, he found that marrying past the early thirties was associated with a slight increase in divorce rates. After thirty-two, each year you wait to tie the knot increases your risk of divorce by 5 percent. That was true regardless of people's education, religion, location, or sexual history.

The data do not offer definitive answers about why this increase in divorce rate occurs, but Wolfinger has some theories. One explanation is that people who really want to get married are likely to have done so by their early thirties—and that group might be more inclined to do what it takes to make their marriage work. Another possible reason is that people who struggle with romantic relationships may delay marriage simply because they kept breaking up with partners in their twenties. "The kinds of people who wait till their thirties to get married may be the kinds of people who aren't predisposed toward doing well in their marriages," Wolfinger says. " . . . More generally, perhaps people who marry later face a pool of potential spouses that has been winnowed down to exclude the individuals most predisposed to succeed at matrimony."[49]

What can we learn from this? For starters, if the data about the ideal marriage window freaked you out, you're probably someone who cares about getting married. This suggests that when you do marry—even if that is well into your thirties or beyond—you will do your best to make the relationship work, especially during rocky periods.

That said, don't hold out for the perfect spouse; that person just does not exist. Any relationship will involve work and compromise, and if you find yourself ending relationships before they have the time to get off the ground, you might miss out on finding a partner who is equally motivated to make the relationship succeed. One more thing: if you're in your rocket years and have noticed that your romantic relationships keep imploding, you might consider seeing a counselor or therapist to get to the root of the problem. If you bring serious relationship issues with you into your thirties, you may have an even harder time finding a spouse.

THE FUTURE OF MARRIAGE

Today's twentysomethings live in a world where marrying their soul mate is not just an aspiration, but a very likely outcome. "Young people have always dreamed of marrying someone they could love," Stephanie Coontz, the historian, said in a recent interview. "But it was so unrealistic, that's why most of the great love stories of history were tragedies."[50]

However, sociologists are finding that not everyone in society is equally able to get married. The marriage data show that wealthy, well-educated Americans are far more likely to wed than are their poorer, less educated peers. That didn't used to be the case. Before the 1970s, the vast majority of Americans got married and stayed married, regardless of social class.[51] But around the 1990s, a great reversal took place.[52] All of a sudden, people who had gone to college married at high rates and those who had not increasingly skipped marriage. Today, 65 percent of college-educated Americans marry, while half of those with a high school diploma or less get married, and this marriage gap is on track to keep widening.

Researchers don't believe that education itself makes people more inclined toward marriage. Instead, they believe the real issue is the growing wealth divide in the United States. College-educated Americans have a higher earning potential, and it is easier to create a lasting, stable, and loving relationship when you have money. With less money, it is harder to throw a wedding, buy a house, and start a family. A recent study found that a third of twentysomething singles say their financial situation has held them back from pursuing love.[53]

The sociologist Victor Chen has observed how people in low-income neighborhoods struggle with marriage.[54] In places where many men are incarcerated, the pool of possible husbands shrinks. Unemployed people, particularly men, aren't perceived to be desirable partners.[55] A recent study found that in towns where factory jobs had disappeared in the 1990s and 2000s, marriage rates dropped.[56] Chen has found that women in these communities sometimes choose to have children even though they can't find the right spouse, which has led to an increase in single moms.

Education and financial stability also seem to make it easier to avoid divorce. In fact, some sociologists now call marriage a luxury good.[57] Among married women, 78 percent of those with college degrees have marriages that last at least two decades, while only 40 percent of those with a high school diploma or less have marriages that last that long.[58] Part of this has to do with the fact that college-educated folks tend to get married older and those additional years give them more maturity to handle conflict.[59] And couples with more resources can afford to get counseling when they hit a roadblock.

Social scientists worry about how these marriage trends will exacerbate the class divide in the country, particularly as the current generation has children.[60] Today, financially stable people are more likely to start families while married, while those who have fewer resources are more likely to have children out of wedlock; 36 percent of children born to working-class moms are born out of wedlock compared to 13 percent of those born to wealthier moms.[61] As we saw earlier in the chapter, children of married parents tend to grow up wealthier than those raised by single parents. We're seeing a vicious cycle play out. "There's a widening gap in access to stable, rewarding relationships," says the historian Stephanie Coontz. "That worries me dreadfully."

However, Coontz also points out that the institution of marriage has always been in flux. Right now, marriage trends are related to the growing economic inequality in the United States. If the country changes course and brings back a thriving middle class, more people may be able to find the happy long-term relationship they desire. "The big question is," Coontz says, "are we going to keep ramping up this economic pressure that is continually tearing down the kinds of strong relationships that people would like to build?"[62]

EVER AFTER

Junes in Atlanta are erratic. They can be hot, humid, and buzzing with mosquitoes. But the day I married Ben, the weather was cool and crisp.

People don't tell you that after months of planning your wedding, the day goes by in a flash. In my memory, my wedding day is a blur of pink and orange, the colors of the bridesmaids' dresses. We were married by my uncle under a wedding chuppah that Ben and his mother had built together a few days before. Alex, my best friend, walked me down the aisle. My father had passed away the year before, but his presence could be felt everywhere on that day, from the sermon his brother gave to the speeches at our reception.

Ben and I tried not to get our outfits messy as we drank too much champagne. My other best friend, Alan, a professional DJ, manned the turntables, playing songs from the sixties and seventies to get the older folks out of their chairs and onto the dance floor. I remember how strange it was seeing people from different parts of our lives all happily mingling together: my cousin hitting it off with Alex; my Singaporean aunt breaking into peals of laughter with Ben's New York uncle.

Then, just like that, the wedding was over. Our guests lined up with sparklers as Ben and I walked down a brick path in the garden hand in hand, then hopped into the car that would take us back to our hotel. When we got to the honeymoon suite, Ben helped me out of the many layers of my heavy silk dress, I kicked off my heels, and we sat on the floor, doing the least romantic thing imaginable: we stuffed our faces with the boxes of food and slices of cake our wedding planner had packed for us. She'd known what she was doing. With all the dancing and catching up with wedding guests, neither of us had eaten much all day. We were famished.

In a lot of ways, that was the moment our marriage began. After years of trying to figure out if we would make good life partners, it felt like such a relief to have settled the question. We had chosen each other as companions for the years ahead. Whatever we did with our lives, we would do it together.

Eight years on, we're still trying to figure all of this out. But the nice thing about marrying someone is that you suddenly have a very long time horizon to make mistakes, pick up the pieces, and do better.

There would be many more dinners eaten on the floor from takeout boxes in the years to come. We'd do it again when we moved to our first home and waited for our furniture to arrive. We'd do it when we brought Ella home from the hospital the day she was born, eating in silence while marveling at our newborn napping on a little cot on the ground. In the end, I've found that these are the moments that make up a marriage.

FIVE

FAMILY

Liz! I'm freezing my eggs! It's time."

Luciana, one of my closest friends, was texting me from Buenos Aires. As the message bubble popped up on my phone, I was on maternity leave, sitting in a rocking chair with one-month-old Ella on my lap. I had finally gotten her to take a nap, so I took advantage of that rare moment of quiet to write back.

> Liz: OMG! OMG! OMG! You are?! 🙌
>
> Luciana: Yup. All my business school friends are doing it. I thought it was a good idea to keep my options open, ya know?

Luciana and I met in San Francisco more than a decade ago through mutual friends. We instantly hit it off, bonding over our shared love of British period dramas and utter bewilderment at American sports. As ambitious women in our early twenties, we spent a lot of our time chatting about how we hoped to make our mark on the world. At the time, I was working to become a professor and she was a consultant with big plans to climb the corporate ladder.

Occasionally, our conversations meandered to the topic of how children—*if* we had them—would fit into the equation. The vast majority of people will eventually become parents: 86 percent of American women will give birth at some point in their life.[1] (It is common for research about family to focus on women because motherhood is much easier to accurately track than fatherhood.) But like many of our peers, Luciana and I did not feel compelled to follow the most common path; neither of us assumed that parenthood was a foregone conclusion.

As we got manicures or went out for a drink, we would wrestle with the question of whether we wanted children at all and if so, when. As it turned out, we had very different impulses. I was in a rush to get pregnant before I turned thirty-five, the age at which everybody from the Mayo Clinic to my mom said my fertility would plummet. Luciana, on the other hand, wanted to devote her twenties and thirties to her career. Of course, neither of us really knew what we were getting ourselves into as we casually discussed our future babies. Most of our friends would not start getting married or having children until their late twenties, so we didn't have very much to go on.

But as uninformed as our choices were, each of us stayed entirely on script, sending us on totally divergent paths. Luciana is now thirty-five. She's just taken a top position at a fast-growing Latin American start-up that requires her to jet between Mexico City, Rio de Janeiro, and Bogotá every month. She's about to start injecting herself with hormones that will enable her to harvest as many eggs as possible in a few weeks. Meanwhile, I am thirty-six, and during my hour-long lunch break, I scramble to Target to locate a pair of *Finding Nemo* goggles for Ella's swimming lessons. (They are apparently all the rage with preschoolers.)

FAMILY PLANNING IN YOUR ROCKET YEARS

Luciana and I were not the only ones who stuck closely to the family plans we had concocted in our twenties. This is, in fact, a common pattern. A 2009 study tracking the same group of American women over forty years found that by their early twenties, most women had a very clear sense of how many children they wanted.[2] And shockingly, the majority of them managed to execute their vision with stunning precision: 67 percent said they wanted two children and gave birth to two babies. Twelve percent wanted three or more children and accomplished that. A smaller group—4 percent—started out wanting two but ended up having one or none at all. For that last group, fertility issues and life events such as getting an advanced degree prompted them to change their plans.

Since the plans we make in our rocket years carry so much weight, it makes sense to spend time thinking about what kind of family will make you happiest. We're fortunate to have more options for creating families than any other generation in history. Here are the decisions before you: First, you should figure out if you want children at all or if you would prefer to skip parenthood. If you decide you do want children, you should consider whether you want biological children or whether you will create a family through adoption, fostering, or surrogacy. And finally, if you decide you want biological children, you can ponder *when* to have them, since there are trade-offs to having children earlier or later in life.

It's valuable to consider your ideal path early, because it will influence other decisions in your life. If you are certain you want a big family or know you don't want children, for instance, you can pick a life partner who shares this goal. If you're already in a serious relationship, you can start a conversation with your significant other about whether you're on the same page and how to work toward common ground. If you're sure you want kids, you might want to take advantage of the years before they arrive to travel or pursue career goals. (Take it from me! Climbing Machu Picchu will be much harder with a toddler!)

While you're thinking all this through, remember that not everything is within our control. Things don't always go according to plan. You might get pregnant unexpectedly. On the flip side, you may have trouble conceiving when you start trying. It might take longer than you hope to find someone to start a family with. All of this will force you to be flexible and resilient. You may have to go back to the drawing board and imagine a different family than the one you had in mind in your early twenties.

But here's the thing: there is no one formula for creating a happy family. There are many ways to cultivate a network of love and support that will carry us through our lives.

WHY DO WE HAVE CHILDREN?

Before we explore the different paths to building a family, it's important to ask a deeper question: Why do we have children at all?

This is a relatively new question in the grand scheme of things. For most of history, humans did not have many choices when it came to family life. Social and religious norms dictated that people marry someone of the opposite sex, then produce children who would continue the lineage, contribute to the household income, and eventually inherit any wealth the family owned. There were also the limits of biology. Until the birth control pill became widely available in the 1960s, sex was inherently tied to reproduction, so any sexual encounter had the potential to lead to a baby. (And perhaps even a shotgun wedding!)

In our own time—thank goodness!—we have much more freedom when it comes to the families we build. Most of us are no longer bound by religious or social duty to procreate. This changes our reasons for starting a family; we do it not out of obligation to anyone else but rather for our own sake. These days, the question of whether to have children comes down to whether we believe they will make us happy or fill our lives with meaning. It's a very personal decision that comes out of our experiences, values, personality, and identity. As a result, one person's motivation to have children will be very different from another's. It's worth mulling over your own desires and articulating them to get a clearer sense of what you want.

For a glimpse into my own thought process, it went something like this. I wanted to experience the wonder of bringing new life into the world. I was eager to watch my baby grow to become an individual with her own imagination and personality. I looked forward to forging a relationship of love, companionship, and trust with that brand-new person. I also believed that raising a child would give me purpose, much like the meaning I derive from my career, marriage, and faith. After my father passed away, I thought there was something beautiful about the fact that his memory still lived on in me and I could pass that memory on to the next generation.

Though the family we create will be largely the result of our idiosyncratic desires and feelings, other external forces influence our thinking as well. Social norms still play a role: data show that we are very susceptible to peer pressure when it comes to family planning. In the 1950s, 65 percent of mothers had three or more children, and it was no coincidence that 71 percent of Americans said that that was the ideal family size.

Fast forward to today: 62 percent of mothers have two children, and now 50 percent of Americans say that this is the ideal family size.[3] Among our generation, there's also a growing trend of choosing to remain child free. In a 2018 survey of 1,858 Americans between the ages of twenty and forty-five, half of respondents hadn't yet had children, and of those, 24 percent said they were sure they did not want kids and another 34 percent had doubts.[4]

Money is another factor. During recessions, people tend to have fewer children because they are not sure they can support them. In the aftermath of the Great Recession in 2008, the birth rate in the United States for women in their twenties dropped by 15 percent.[5] But even when the economy is good, the rising cost of giving birth to a baby and raising a child are big considerations. Delivering a baby in the United States without complications costs about $30,000.[6] Raising a child until the age of eighteen costs a whopping $230,000.[7] It's downright astronomical! Many Americans say that money is the main reason for having fewer kids than they would like.[8]

And although we refer to babies as bundles of joy, there is mounting evidence that kids actually make parents less happy, at least according to some psychological measures of happiness.[9] People with children often report lower levels of marital satisfaction and mental well-being.[10] As a frazzled mother of a small child who barely has time to see my husband, this is something I can relate to. For some people this is enough of an argument not to have children at all. (But more on that soon.)

These child-free folks have a point. I can attest that babies sometimes make you less happy than you were before they showed up. Ben and I don't get as much sleep as we need, the cost of child care strains our budget, and we're both struggling to stay on top of our careers. On the other hand, Ella has given us new joys, even in our tired, bedraggled state. We love watching her take in the world for the first time, marveling at the flowers in the garden or the way the sky turns pink before sunset. It's wonderful hearing her laugh when we read her favorite book before bedtime. In the words of the author Jennifer Senior, the paradox of modern parenthood is that it is "all joy and no fun."[11]

RACING AGAINST THE BIOLOGICAL CLOCK

By choosing to have a baby and doing so in our early thirties, Ben and I represented a common path when it comes to building a family. Over the last few decades, women have been increasingly choosing to delay motherhood. The average American woman now has her first baby between the ages of twenty-six and thirty, depending on her level of education. Those in bigger cities or with a postgraduate degree tend to wait until their early thirties.[12] For many people, the goal is to squeeze in their pregnancies before their midthirties, when age-related fertility issues begin to kick in.

That was our story. After Ben and I married at twenty-nine, we felt as though we were in a race against my biological clock. We scrambled to get our careers in order and save money for the expenses a baby would generate, which are, as we have just seen, gargantuan.[13] Given the organized, meticulous people we are, we created budgets and checklists and timelines. At thirty-two, I started tracking my ovulation cycle and taking prenatal vitamins. "We are going to rock this pregnancy thing," I remember telling Ben before giving him a high five.

Oh, how wrong I was. We were about to discover that nothing about parenthood is neat and tidy. The reality kicked in shortly after we tried to conceive for the first time. I got pregnant almost immediately, but I started bleeding a few weeks in, and it was clear that I was miscarrying. We had heard that pregnancy losses are common, with average rates as high as 15 percent and the risk going up as you get older.[14] Yet when it happened to us, we were devastated. The experience made us realize that the path to having a baby would be far more unpredictable and terrifying than we had imagined.

I eventually got pregnant again, this time with Ella. From the start, it became clear that I was losing control of my own body. Things tasted and smelled different, I had to pee every twenty minutes around the clock, and I was always tired. Ella had a mind of her own there in my belly. She would make little fluttering movements and gently prod me with her tiny foot throughout the day. When I entered my third trimester, things got even more dramatic. I had a lot of difficulty breathing, and my doctor told me I would need a C-section. At the time, I didn't fully understand that the procedure would require cutting open my abdominal muscles and temporarily dislodging my stomach to take out the baby. Lovely. But then, a few weeks later, Ella was in the world. And she was perfect. From the moment she emerged from my womb, she had the most expressive face I had ever seen in an infant. Ben and I were overwhelmed with love. We had willed our family into existence.

In my twenties, I had no real sense of how a baby would disrupt my life. Taking care of a newborn was the hardest thing I have done. Ben was as supportive as possible, doing most of Ella's diaper changes and the domestic chores. But for all our feminist beliefs, we realized that there are some things that only a mother can do, especially in the earliest days. I couldn't walk or move comfortably for six weeks after the C-section, but

I still had to figure out how to breastfeed to keep Ella alive. I had a few meltdowns in those early weeks of motherhood, when both Ella and I burst into tears and poor Ben looked on, bewildered.

I was particularly unprepared for the way motherhood would turn my career upside down. In the years before I gave birth to Ella, I had found my dream job writing for a magazine. I had thrown myself into my work, writing late into the night and reporting multiple stories at once. But after I returned from maternity leave, I was lucky to get the bare minimum done. Every hour I wasn't working was consumed with taking care of Ella. If she got sick and could not go to day care, I had to take the day off work. I turned down speaking engagements and assignments in other cities because it just felt too exhausting to travel. One time I had an opportunity to interview Tiger Woods in New York, so Ben took time off work and we brought six-month-old Ella with us on Amtrak. It was such a nightmare that it turned me off business trips for another six months. All of that happened right when my career should have been taking off. I was establishing myself as a writer, and I was working toward bigger, more ambitious projects. I wanted to start turning one of my many book ideas into reality. But instead, I was topless in my home office, attached to a terribly designed breast pump, barely treading water at my job.

There's a term for this struggle. Sociologists describe the systematic disadvantages that mothers experience in the workplace as the "motherhood penalty." Over the last few decades, the workplace has become a far more even playing field for women, but as soon as a woman has a baby, she starts falling behind her male colleagues, making less money and getting promoted less often. This happens because mothers are more likely to reduce their work hours, take time off, turn down a promotion, or quit their job to care for their children than fathers.[15] And even when both parents have a full-time job, mothers spend almost twice as much time on housework and childcare as fathers do.[16] All of this adds up to a big wage gap between men and women. The Census Bureau has found that working mothers earn 75 percent of what their male counterparts make.[17]

New moms experience many forms of discrimination. Mothers are stereotyped as bad employees, and companies penalize them simply for having children. A Stanford study found that mothers were deemed to be 10 percent less competent and 12.1 percent less committed to their jobs than nonmothers among otherwise equal candidates.[18] Childless women were also 8.2 times as likely to be recommended for a promotion and 6 times as likely to be recommended for a job as mothers. And get this: mothers were held to higher punctuality standards than nonmothers were. They could be late on average only 3.16 days a month before it negatively impacted them, while their childless colleagues could be late 3.73 days. No matter how devoted they are to their jobs, moms just can't get a break.

As if things couldn't be any more unfair, the study found that fathers are deemed to be 5 percent more committed to their work than nonfathers! Yeah, I know, it's ridiculous! Fathers were allowed to have more late days than nonfathers (3.6 days versus 3.16 days) before they were penalized for it. Sociologists believe that this double standard comes down to the fact that men are seen as breadwinners. Once they have children, they are perceived to be even more devoted to their jobs because they need to support their family. Mothers, on the other hand, are still seen as caregivers, so children are perceived to be a distraction from their work.

Experts say that it will take a long time to undo these problematic stereotypes and wage discrepancies. There are several systemic changes that need to occur before this can happen.

The government could provide subsidized or free child care and make paid parental leave a right. Companies could implement policies such as giving employees flexibility about when and where they work and make it easier for women to jump back into their work after taking time off to have and care for children. And it would help if men took time off after their children were born and spent more time on child care. But until that time comes, women who choose to have children in their late twenties and early thirties will continue to face big hurdles in the workplace.

TO FREEZE OR NOT TO FREEZE

> Liz: OK, so when did you start thinking about egg-freezing?
> Luciana: A few years ago. It came up a lot in business school.
> Liz: Makes sense. You're making a big investment in your career.
> Luciana: Yeah, and you want to maximize your return. The first years post-MBA are super important. Freezing your eggs de-risks the decision to be childless.

Luciana was trained as an economist and often talks through complex life events using economic frameworks. It's one of the things I love most about her. Whenever I've had a big decision to make, such as whether to break up with someone or quit a job, I have found it so comforting to hear her break down the issue rationally and help me think through what I really want.

Luciana loves babies and came to visit Ella when she was just a few months old, showering her with presents and kisses. But when it comes to starting her own family, she's able to compartmentalize her emotions and process the decision logically. Part of the reason she decided to delay pregnancy is because of research showing that women who have their first baby after the age of thirty-five tend to experience less of the motherhood penalty because they are more established in their careers. As a result, these slightly older mothers don't take as much of a salary hit and seem better able to keep rising in their industries.[19] Luciana has already invested a lot of time and money into her career, so she thinks it makes sense to work for a bit longer and get a few more promotions before having a baby.

The problem is that thirty-five also happens to be the year that we are told that our fertility drops off a cliff. This isn't entirely accurate. Back in the late 1980s, doctors discovered that the chance of having a baby with Down syndrome was about 1 in 200 for a woman aged thirty-five. Coincidentally, amniocentesis, the procedure used to check if a baby had Down syndrome, carried a 1-in-200 chance of miscarriage. In other words, the risk of having a baby with a chromosomal disorder at thirty-five was the same as the risk of miscarriage due to identifying that very disorder. The thing is, these figures are no longer valid. Thanks to advancements in medical technology, a thirty-five-year-old's chances of giving birth to a baby with Down syndrome is 1 in 350, while 1 in 1,600 women will experience miscarriage due to amniocentesis.[20] Yet the medical system continues to refer to pregnant women over the age of thirty-five as "geriatric." (As if they didn't feel bad enough!)

That said, it's true that women are up against a very real biological clock. Women are born with a fixed number of eggs, and their body releases one or two every month from the time they reach puberty until menopause. It is harder to conceive as they get older because they ovulate less frequently. One large study found that the probability of pregnancy following sex on the most fertile day of a woman's menstrual cycle was 40 percent in women aged twenty-seven to thirty-four, but that went down to 30 percent in women thirty-five to thirty-nine.[21] It's a shift for sure, but it's not as though our chances of getting pregnant disappear on our thirty-fifth birthday. Fertility doctors say that by the time a woman reaches her early forties, it becomes very hard to have a baby with her own eggs. And that's not all: as women head into their late thirties, they are at higher risk of many other issues, from miscarriage to stillbirth to premature delivery.[22]

Some of these problems can be solved by egg freezing. We're the first generation of women to have this option. The first-ever baby born from frozen eggs was delivered in Singapore in 1986. For decades afterward, the procedure seemed bizarre and futuristic. In the early 2000s, doctors began offering it as an option to women about to undergo chemotherapy, which can be toxic for eggs, but it wasn't until 2012 that the American Society for Reproductive Medicine formally removed it from the list of "experimental" procedures.[23] Over the last few years, many egg-freezing clinics have popped up, but since the technology is new, it is still expensive. One round of egg retrieval costs about $10,000, and most doctors recommend going through two or three to have the best chance of having a baby.

In 2014, when Luciana was in business school, the conversation about egg freezing hit the mainstream. That was partly because Facebook announced that it would help employees and their spouses cover up to $20,000 in egg-freezing expenses, which amounts to about two rounds of egg retrieval. That sparked a lot of debate. Critics made the case that egg-freezing benefits are ultimately designed to help a company's bottom line, since women will be able to devote more time to their work in their twenties and thirties. Some suggested that Facebook was effectively putting pressure on women to delay childbearing, which should be a personal decision. Facebook defended itself by saying that it was a policy that employees themselves had requested.

When Luciana and her classmates, who were pouring hundreds of thousands of dollars into a professional degree, talked it over, they generally thought that Facebook's policy was fantastic. It gave women more control over their careers, removing the pressure to have children during their most productive years. And given how expensive the procedure was, it would spare them a lot of money. Over the last few years, other companies, including Chanel, the law firm Ropes & Gray, and the consulting firm Bain & Company, have added egg freezing as an employee benefit. And experts believe it will become increasingly common in the years to come.

Though some women like the idea of egg freezing because it allows them to focus on their work, others simply haven't met the person they want to settle down with by their midthirties. A 2018 study showed that 85 percent of women who freeze their eggs are single, and half said that it was uncertainty about when they would find a partner that had brought them to the clinic. The next largest group had been driven there by divorce or a breakup. Among those in relationships, many said that their partner's unwillingness to have a baby immediately had made them decide to go through with the procedure.[24]

Many women see egg freezing as an insurance policy that will allow them to have a baby even after their fertility begins to decline. But the procedure doesn't guarantee being able to conceive. A recent study by the Human Fertilisation and Embryology Authority in the United Kingdom found that of women who had used frozen eggs in 2016, only 19 percent of implantation cycles had led to pregnancy.[25] The chances of success depend on many factors, including age. A Harvard Medical School study from 2017 found that the chance of a live birth decreased depending on the age the woman was when she froze them. Women who froze twenty eggs at twenty-eight had a 94 percent chance of having a live birth, but those who froze the same number of eggs at thirty-seven or forty-two only had a 75 percent and 37 percent chance of having a live birth respectively.[26]

Doctors believe that egg-freezing technology will continue to improve, which will lead to better success rates. And as the procedure becomes more common, it will also become cheaper, allowing more women to do it. At some point, it might be the norm for women in their early twenties to freeze their eggs as a backup plan, so they'll be able to have a baby no matter how their lives unfold.

> Luciana: I think egg-freezing will be the top graduation present in a decade from now.
> Liz: I'll remember that when Ella graduates.
> Luciana: Yes, Aunty Lu will buy her a new suit and a round of egg retrieval.

A CHILD-FREE LIFE

I have a distinct memory of Andrew at twenty-five. He looked like some sort of Californian Adonis, with long locks of golden hair that fell around his face. He spent weekends camping or hitting the beach, but he wasn't your average surfer dude; he was a student at San Francisco Theological Seminary, preparing for a career as a pastor. Most Presbyterian ministers I knew were married with gaggles of kids. But that wasn't the future Andrew had in mind for himself. He wanted a quiet life, full of reading and long walks. He was perfectly happy never to hear the pitter-patter of little feet in his home.

Andrew and I were crossing the street in Berkeley one evening when he mentioned that he was pretty sure he didn't want kids. I was twenty-four at the time, and that took me by surprise. I had never met anyone who spoke with such confidence about not wanting to have kids. Soon after our conversation, Andrew met Holly, his future wife, at a wilderness camp where they were both counselors. They bonded over their faith, their mutual enjoyment of nature, and—crucially—their desire to remain childless. Holly loves children. She's spent most of her career as a teacher. But she's also seen firsthand how few parents actually give their children the attention they need. So she, like Andrew, decided that she would skip becoming a parent.

Over the last few decades, the number of childless people in American society has fluctuated between about 15 and 20 percent of the population. About 10 percent of people will encounter fertility problems that may prevent them from having children. But a growing number of people are not having children entirely by choice. Economists have found that childlessness has been rising among wealthy and highly educated people, suggesting that people in this category aren't remaining childless due to lack of resources.[27]

In a recent study conducted by the *New York Times* and the market research firm Morning Consult, about 12 percent of 1,858 survey respondents between the ages of twenty and forty-five said they did not want to have children, and 17 percent said they weren't sure. There were many reasons for wanting to remain childless. About a third said they simply had no desire for children, while a quarter said they were not sure they would be good parents. A full 36 percent said they wanted to have more leisure time. On the other hand, 18 percent wanted to focus on their careers, and 14 percent said they worked too much to handle the demands of having children.[28]

It's not easy to commit to a childless life. American society still has fairly traditional views when it comes to family. Sociologists describe children as an important source of "social capital" that helps us deepen our ties to our community. New babies have a way of bringing families closer, as grandparents and siblings show up for celebrations or help babysit.[29] And friendship circles often shift as people get married and have children. Single people and childless couples often have trouble socializing with their friends who have children because these parents are often so distracted and consumed by their family responsibilities.

It can also be hard to push back against deeply entrenched beliefs that children are necessary to pass on our name and genes to the next generation, allowing us to live on in some form after we die. Since having children is such a widespread norm, people often feel the need to defend their choice to be childless to their friends and family. This is particularly true for Andrew, who spends most of his days in Christian communities, which tend to have a more conservative concept of what a family unit should look like.

In sociological research, scholars have found many reasons that people choose to remain childless. The kind of people who choose this path tend to derive deep satisfaction from their work and have high aspirations for their careers. People who say they don't want kids are often in happy romantic partnerships that provide them with meaning and emotional satisfaction.[30] But it can be hard to generalize about what drives people to skip parenthood. It's a personal decision based on idiosyncratic reasons.

One day, I sat down with Andrew and Holly to talk to them about why they had decided not to become parents. By now they are experts at explaining their thought process and can boil down their decision to two reasons. First, they believe that giving life to a human being is a sacred act, and raising someone to be a kind, decent person is incredibly challenging. Many people have children to feel complete, but Andrew and Holly believe that we shouldn't have children for what they can give to us but rather for what we can give to them. "Ultimately, I think that society is asking the wrong question," Andrew says. "We should not be interrogating people who do not want kids; we should be interrogating those who do."

Secondly, as environmentalists, Andrew and Holly think a lot about how humans are systematically destroying the planet. They're vegetarian, own as little as possible, recycle obsessively, and avoid using a car. But for all those efforts, they say that not having a child is the single most impactful decision they will ever make to protect the earth and fight climate change. A study by Environmental Research Letters found that having one fewer child will save 58.6 tons of CO_2 per year (not having a car will save only 2.4 tons a year while eating a plant-based diet will save 0.82 tons), to say nothing of the diapers, plastic toys, clothes, and food a kid will require.

All those reasons served to convince Andrew that people should think carefully about the impact that having just one child has on the planet. This reasoning is becoming increasingly common: 14 percent of those who don't want children or aren't sure say they are worried about overpopulation, and 11 percent have concerns about climate change.[31] A group of millennials from around the world are so concerned about global warming that they have launched what they call a birthstrike, promising not to have any children until global leaders work toward fixing the climate crisis.

It was important to Andrew that he figure these issues out in his twenties because it would influence whom he dated or married. Researchers have found that some marriages end in divorce because spouses have diverging expectations about having children.[32] Sometimes they differ on how many children to have; in other cases, they disagree about whether to have children at all. The desire to have a child can be overwhelming. Psychologists say that involuntarily childless men and women report a sense of loss, depression, exclusion, and isolation and tend to indulge in more risk-taking behaviors.[33] Some couples don't address the issue of children before the relationship gets serious, either because they assume that all people want children or because one or both parties hasn't yet decided what he or she wants. This miscommunication can lead to a great deal of conflict and pain.

Andrew now serves as a pastor of a small congregation in the Pacific Northwest, and Holly works as a wilderness guide. They have more space in their lives—both literal and figurative—for other people. They regularly invite friends to their home for gatherings or extended visits. Their lives are full, but in a very different way from mine, which Ella has littered with building blocks, cookie crumbs, and onesies covered in spit-up.

THE MYRIAD WAYS WE CAN BUILD FAMILIES
IN THE MODERN WORLD

Unlike Andrew, another friend of mine, Ben (not to be confused with my husband), knew with certainty that he wanted to be a father. We met as graduate students at Berkeley, and even then, he spoke fondly about one day having a family. But neither of us fully grasped how hard it would be for him to make that happen as a gay man. There are 4.3 percent of US adults (or 10.7 million) who identify as gay, lesbian, or transgender.[34] As of 2017, a full 10 percent of all LGBTQ adults are married to a same-sex partner, and that figure is rising, but these couples face enormous hurdles when it comes to having children.[35]

Ben and his partner, Chris, just celebrated the first birthday of their son, Roman. Little Roman is 1 of approximately 200,000 children being raised by a same-sex couple.[36] Since our children are only a year apart, Ben and I sometimes trade notes on parenthood. He sends me pictures of Roman napping on the couch. I send him pictures of Ella going down a slide. It's all the typical sappy stuff you'd expect of besotted parents of toddlers. But whereas my journey to giving birth to Ella was fairly straightforward (and covered by insurance), Ben had to spend years and most of his savings to bring Roman into the world.

Ben now advises other members of the LGBTQ community to consider the possibility of children early, because not only will you need to find a partner who shares your vision for a family, you will likely have to put aside a lot of money to make it happen. He says there are plenty of unforeseen costs that go along with being an LGBTQ parent, whether you choose to create a family by adoption, fostering, or surrogacy.

On their third date, Ben asked Chris three questions in order of importance: Did he want to be monogamous? Did he want to have a baby? And was he willing to go hiking regularly? (Ben loves hiking. That was nonnegotiable.) Chris said yes to all three, and within a year, they were thinking about how best to have a child. The couple first planned to foster or adopt, as do many of their LGBTQ peers. (Same-sex couples are six times as likely to foster children and at least four times as likely to adopt as their non-LGBTQ counterparts.)[37] They had heard that optics matter a great deal to US adoption agencies, so before they even began the adoption process, they tried to ensure that their lives mimicked a straight couple's as much as possible; they bought a house in a residential neighborhood of Seattle, full of other families.

But even after doing that, they discovered that the adoption system can be biased against LGBTQ people. Outside the United States, many countries, particularly those in Africa and Asia, explicitly forbid gay couples to adopt. In the United States, the 2015 ruling that upheld the right to same-sex marriage also made same-sex adoption legal. However, in practice, adoption agencies can discriminate against same-sex couples in implicit ways. Some deny LGBTQ couples by finding arbitrary problems during home visits, or simply deprioritizing them on lists. Ben and Chris tried their best to work within the system, but they kept running into hurdles.

In the end, they decided to take the surrogacy route. But that approach raised many ethical questions for them, as it does for many gay couples.[38] At what point was surrogacy a form of coercion? If a woman was in a dire financial situation, was she voluntarily choosing to carry someone else's baby? Or was she sacrificing her body because she had little other choice? Ben and Chris spent many late nights pondering that question. The solution, they felt, was to find a surrogate who seemed as though she didn't need the money and would actually enjoy the experience of pregnancy.

Only nineteen states currently allow surrogacy to married same-sex couples, and in another fifteen states, same-sex couples can do it only because no law actively prohibits it.[39] The surrogate Ben and Chris found lived in Los Angeles, which was ideal because California happens to have progressive laws for same-sex couples using surrogacy.[40] "This woman in question is a preschool teacher and has a sixteen-year-old daughter. She had already carried a set of twins previously as a surrogate. She liked the idea of helping other people make the families they couldn't create on their own. She told us, 'Every year, I get a new batch of three-year-olds in my classroom,'" Ben explained. "'I have a wonderful year with them, and love them, and teach them how to survive in the world. Then I say good-bye to them, and let them go onto their next teacher. That's how I feel about being a surrogate: I carry the baby for nine months; then I let the baby go on to their next stage in life.'"

Though about 750 children a year are born via surrogate in the United States, surrogacy is still considered controversial in many places.[41] Most European countries and some US states have banned it on ethical grounds, whether the surrogate is paid for the transaction or does it altruistically. In states where surrogacy is legal, surrogates can earn a fee starting at $20,000 per child, and more experienced surrogates can earn a lot more.[42] The younger the surrogate, the better the chances of her successfully carrying the baby to term. Surrogacy agencies commonly require women who want to be surrogates to have already had a baby, partly so they are fully aware of what lies ahead. Women in their twenties who meet that precondition are highly desirable surrogates, since they're young, healthy, and likely to have a successful pregnancy. One study about surrogacy found that the average age of a surrogate is twenty-eight. She's usually married, often with two to three biological children of her own, and with a household income of less than $60,000.[43]

Choosing the right surrogate was just the first of many complex decisions Ben and Chris had to make. Their next question was what combination of sperm and egg to use. Both men have sisters, and all were willing to donate their eggs to help them have a baby. In the end, they decided to go with Ben's sperm and Chris's sister's egg. The sister went through an egg retrieval process similar to the one that Luciana experienced, but rather than freezing only the egg, the doctors froze an embryo created from the sperm and the egg, which they eventually implanted into the surrogate's womb.

This procedure cost close to $130,000, including the surrogate fee, insurance, egg retrieval, and embryo freezing. Ben and Chris had to hire three separate lawyers: one for themselves, one representing the surrogate, and one representing Chris's sister. Those costs added up. Chris works in tech, and his employer happened to have very progressive fertility benefits, offering $13,500 in cash to any staff member who wanted to freeze eggs or adopt. "We were so grateful for the help," said Ben. "But at the same time, it's sad that this is just a drop in the bucket." Fortunately, both Chris and Ben had foreseen the huge expense and had been saving up for years. And all of that loving preparation led to little Roman, who is now an expert mountaineer, thanks to his dads, who tote him around in a Baby Bjorn through the mountains of Washington State.

I've always found it inspiring hearing the stories of LGBTQ parents. Many, like Ben and Chris, have had to overcome enormous hurdles in their quest to build a family. But their experiences reveal something profound about the human desire to forge lifelong bonds with other people. As I was writing this chapter, I spoke with Trystan Reese, the director of family formation at the Family Equality Council, an organization that promotes equality for LGBTQ families. He was one of the first trans men who publicly shared his journey of being visibly pregnant and having a baby. His family received a lot of hate

mail during that period, along with many letters of encourage-
ment. But Trystan still felt it was important to share his story,
because it could help many other people rethink their idea of
what a family could look like.

Through his work, he has seen the myriad ways that people
build families in the modern world. Thanks to new technologies
and changing social norms, we now have more freedom to build
families in creative ways. Sometimes this means depending on
new medical developments, such as egg freezing or surrogacy.
Sometimes it means caring for other people's children through
adoption or fostering. Sometimes it simply involves choosing to
live in a tight-knit community, where people love and support
one another.

"The desire to create a family can feel, and be, limitless,"
Trystan told me. "Some of us do have this need inside of us to
create systems of support and love around us, and family is one
really great way to do that."

I'm not sure I fully understood what it meant to build such
a system of love and support until I gave birth to Ella. I always
imagined that parenthood was about pouring yourself into your
child, supporting her, and giving her everything you have. And
it certainly is all those things. But I didn't realize how eager my
little Ella would be to offer support and empathy to us, as well.
Something changed in Ben and me when we brought Ella home
from the hospital. The two of us had been a couple for more
than a decade at that point, but with Ella, we suddenly became
something more powerful: a community.

SIX

FRIENDSHIP

For five years, I lived with my two best friends, Alan and Alex, in a small house in Berkeley. The place was a little crummy, with paper-thin walls and ugly linoleum floors. But what we lacked in interior design, we made up for in midnight heart-to-hearts over beer and ice cream. We had a tradition of gathering in the kitchen late at night like some sort of tribal council to go over the latest drama in our love lives. Why, for instance, had Alan come back from a date covered in cat hair the other night? We needed the full story. Should I go on a second date with a guy who spontaneously broke into song, as if he were in a musical? The council firmly voted no.

The three of us had fallen into our friendship entirely by chance. We were each about to start graduate programs at UC Berkeley: Alan in archaeology, Alex in psychology, and myself in Indian literature. Given our minuscule teaching salaries, it made sense to share a three-bedroom apartment with roommates. We found one another, as one does, through a Craigslist ad. When we met up for the first time, we liked one another instantly.

We quickly settled into a shared life. As the only early bird in the group, I learned to postpone my peppy morning chatter until at least 9:00 a.m. I stayed clear of the guys when they returned from their daily weight-lifting session, sweat dripping down their 1970s-style headbands. I made fun of Alex's protein shakes and Alan's habit of eating an entire box of Trader Joe's mochi ice cream in one sitting. They were astonished at how my beauty products slowly took over the entire bathroom. (Alan: "She has a scrub just for her toes, Alex! HER TOES!") Through our years of cooking together, grocery shopping, walking to class, and picking each other up from the doctor, we became a kind of family.

In the end, I was the one who broke up our little trio when I moved out of our shared home at the age of twenty-six. And just as the data predicted, that was when my circle of friends began to shrink.

I had been mulling over the move for weeks. I was worried about the mountain of work before me in my last year of grad school. Living down the hall from my two favorite people seemed like a recipe for distraction. It was too easy to procrastinate by asking Alan to go on a midnight ice cream run or rewatching *The Matrix* with Alex. They nodded with understanding as I told them my plan one night at our favorite Japanese restaurant. We were all edging toward the end of our graduate programs. This moment was inevitable.

A few months later, I signed a lease for a studio close to campus with wood floors and plenty of shelves for my books. The guys found a two-bedroom high-rise apartment to rent in downtown Oakland. And of course, they helped me with every step of the move. They barely trusted me to drive my VW bug around Berkeley, so there was no way in hell they were going to let me maneuver a moving truck by myself. Alan drove the

U-Haul. Alex helped me load the vehicle with all my earthly possessions. When we got to my new home, the guys carried in my furniture, while I carefully carried in my desk lamp and wine glasses. And just like that, we were done.

It wasn't such a drastic move, really; they would be only a few minutes away. We would see each other all the time, they promised. But after they hugged me and left, I sat on the beautiful wood floor of my studio, surrounded by bare walls and a pile of books, and sobbed. I would miss Alan sauntering around in a fuzzy bathrobe and slippers, sleepily brushing his teeth in the morning. It would never again be so easy to tell Alex about how my mom was driving me crazy.

I was right to be sad. Over the next few years, I found myself spending less and less time with friends, and for a social butterfly like me, that was terrifying. When Ben and I got engaged at the age of twenty-eight, I moved across the country to be with him in Boston, leaving my entire network of friends in California. I kept in touch with Alan and Alex, but more peripheral friends fell off my radar. The years that followed were a blur of wedding planning, hustling at my job, and having a baby. By the time I came up for air in my early thirties, I discovered I hadn't made a new close friend in years.

This is a common pattern when it comes to twentysomething friendships. Most people lose a third of their friends between their midtwenties and midthirties. The truth is that it's very hard to make and keep friends as an adult. This has been a big topic of conversation for the last few years, particularly among older millennials who woke up in their thirties to find they had few friends left. Part of this collective concern is that medical researchers have discovered that friends matter more to our health and well-being than they previously realized. People with friends have lower rates of chronic illness, higher resistance to pain, and longer lives. Loneliness, on the other hand, is as lethal as smoking fifteen cigarettes a day.[1] Yet more than half of Americans feel isolated, and twentysomethings report feeling lonelier than older generations.[2] This is scary stuff. But the important thing to remember is that it is possible to make and deepen friendships at any point in your life.

YOUR TWENTIES ARE A MAGICAL FRIEND-MAKING TIME

Bill Rawlins, a scholar of friendship, says our rocket years are "the golden age for forming friendships."[3] In our twenties, we get our first taste of adult friendships, which are more complex and meaningful than our childhood ones. We also have more time than ever to nurture and deepen these relationships. One of the most beautiful qualities of friendships is that they are voluntary: we choose to love and support our friends. But friendships are also more fragile than other relationships in our lives, since we don't make formal commitments to our friends. Whereas social norms dictate that you live with your spouse and care for your child, no fixed pattern guarantees that a friendship will keep chugging along. Some friends can go days, weeks, months, or years without contact, then pick up just where they left off.

Psychologists highlight the fluidity and variation in these relationships, but say they are generally characterized by mutuality and equal exchange. Friends like each other, open up to each other, and provide each other with emotional and tangible support.[4] Researchers have found that, as with love, there is such a thing as "friendship at first sight." Humor, in particular, is a great predictor of whether two people will have chemistry. This was true with Alan, Alex, and me: we cracked each other up the first time we met. This makes sense because what you find funny says a lot about your personality, intelligence, and beliefs. Much like married couples, friends generally share similarities along several dimensions, including demographic traits, intelligence, personality, attitudes, beliefs, and hobbies.[5] And people who project empathy, warmth, and interest are seen as better friend material.[6] No surprises here. Who wants to be friends with the grumpy-looking guy standing in the corner at a party?

Our twenties are an important time to invest in friendships for two reasons. First, you will have many opportunities to meet like-minded people in these years, and second, you have the time to nurture relationships. In your twenties, your life is in flux, which means you'll find yourself surrounded by new people due to changes in your school, work, and living arrangements. This gives you the opportunity to create a rich network of friends, ranging from close confidants to distant connections. How intimate these relationships will become depends on how much time you spend on them: it takes fifty hours of personal interaction to go from being an acquaintance to being a superficial friend and another forty hours to solidify that bond. It takes a total of two hundred hours of spending time together for friends to feel close.[7]

How many friends in each category can you expect to have in your adult life?[8] It's really up to you. Social scientists have found that social networks vary from 250 to 5,500 people, though the majority of these contacts will be distant, casual, and low stakes.[9] You should not discount people at the outer edges of your circle, because they can play an important role in your life, as I will explain shortly. But when it comes to intimate relationships, your circle of friends will be much smaller. On average, people have 121 friends they care enough about to contact at least once a year, usually during the holidays,[10] but only

10 to 20 people they trust.[11] And they have only two confidants in whom they can really confide.[12]

More than a decade after I first met Alan and Alex, they are still my best friends. After I moved into my own place, I still saw them all the time, as they had promised. Then, two years later, we spread out across the country. Alex stayed in San Francisco, Alan moved to Los Angeles, and I moved to Boston. By then our friendship was strong enough that we could keep our bond alive through texts, emails, and the occasional meetup. When my father passed away, Alan and Alex flew to London to be with my family for his funeral. (They knew my father well from the many times he had come to visit me in Berkeley.) When Ben and I married a few years later, they were by my side. Alex even walked me down the aisle.

YOUR CIRCLE OF FRIENDS WILL SHRINK AT AGE TWENTY-FIVE

The Bureau of Labor Statistics has found that the amount of time we spend with friends peaks at age twenty-five, when we spend about three hours a day with them. But this decreases slowly for the next decade, until around age thirty-five, when the typical American spends an hour a day with friends.[13] The amount of time we spend alone increases steadily throughout our lives. Depressing, I know. By the time we're in our eighties, we will spend nearly eight hours a day alone. That's when I'm planning to finally get through my Netflix queue.

It's not just that we spend less time socializing; the number of friends in our social circle declines, too. Researchers have found that the number of friends that we contact on a regular basis peaks at the age of twenty-five, at about eighteen friends.

Immediately thereafter, our circle begins to shrink.[14] By the time we're forty, we have only twelve close friends, and by eighty, we have seven.

Why the sudden friend drop-off in our midtwenties? Marriage and children are the biggest culprits. As we have seen, most Americans start families in their late twenties and early thirties. These relationships tend to displace friendships. Even if you choose to stay single or child free, it can be hard to maintain close relationships with friends who have become parents. (Mea culpa! I promise to reply to all my friends' emails more regularly as soon as Ella is potty trained!) And as I mentioned, friendships can dissolve more easily than family relationships, which have a more formal structure.

Our friendships also suffer in our late twenties because we move frequently. People between the ages of twenty-five and twenty-nine migrate to another state at a higher rate than any other age group.[15] One study found that college graduates are more likely to move for work, resulting in more dispersed circles of friends.[16] It is much harder to deepen long-distance friendships. Psychologists have found that face-to-face interaction matters a lot early in friendships, but after building a foundation you can feel close to friends even if you cannot connect with them as frequently.[17] If a friendship lacks that initial bond, it will weaken—and even disintegrate—with distance.

Having fewer friends is not entirely a bad thing. As we focus on other important priorities in life, such as family and career, it makes sense to be more selective about whom we bring into our lives. With age, we are better equipped to identify people who might be toxic or harmful, so we can weed them out. Some scholars have found that even though older people have fewer friends and spend less time with them, their friendships can sometimes be more emotionally satisfying. "As people age and time horizons grow shorter, people invest in what is most important, typically meaningful relationships, and derive increasingly greater satisfaction from these investments," one study revealed.[18]

WHY FRIENDS MATTER

The problem, though, is that most Americans don't feel satisfied with their friendships. A 2018 study of twenty thousand Americans identified twentysomethings as a particularly lonely cohort.[19] Using an established scoring system called the UCLA Loneliness Scale (oof, how sad is that?), the researchers found that Gen Zers had the highest loneliness score, followed by millennials. And as we have seen, most of these twentysomethings will lose friends in the years to come. Across the board, Americans do not fare well when it comes to loneliness. More than half of the respondents said that no one knew them well. More than 40 percent said they felt alone and isolated. A third said they had no one to turn to in times of grief or trouble. Figures like these really freak me out.

Doctors appear to be equally worried. Some have declared that a loneliness epidemic is taking over the country and becoming a public health crisis. Loneliness appears to be one of the main triggers for mental health problems.[20] It may even be responsible for the spike in suicide rates and drug overdoses in the United States.[21] Friendlessness can also take a toll on your body. One meta-analysis found that feeling lonely has the same impact on mortality as being obese or chain-smoking.[22]

But let's look at the more positive side of the story. Having close friends can boost your immune system, increase your body's ability to handle pain,[23] and serve as a predictor of happiness levels.[24] As people get older, their friendships will have a bigger influence on their health than even their family relationships do. One large-scale study found that prioritizing friendships resulted in better physical health, while prioritizing family relationships seemed to have no impact.[25] It's making me think that perhaps Alan, Alex, and I should plan to move into the same retirement home together.

All of these studies focused on our closest friendships. But more distant, casual friendships also matter. Sociologists use the term "weak ties" to refer to people who know each other but do not feel deeply emotionally connected.[26] A weak tie could be anyone from a person you see from time to time at the gym to a favorite barista at your neighborhood coffee joint. These low-stakes relationships make people feel connected to their community, which also increases happiness and sense of belonging,[27] overall life satisfaction,[28] and the capacity for empathy.[29] Though you may not turn to these more peripheral friends for emotional support, they can often help you in tangible ways, such as connecting you to job opportunities. So there you have it: say good morning to your neighbors when you head out to work in the morning. It's more rewarding than you think!

PROJECT: MAKE A FRIEND

At thirty-four, I was suddenly thrust into a situation where I had no choice but to make new friends. After a long time in grad school, Ben finally finished *his* PhD. He applied to positions across the country, and as luck would have it, he landed a great job as a professor. In . . . Tallahassee, Florida. To be perfectly honest, as someone who hadn't grown up in the United States, I could not locate Tallahassee on a map. But wherever it was,

I wasn't thrilled about the move. We didn't know a soul in Florida.

"We'll just have to make new friends," Ben said, trying to be comforting.

"But how?" I asked him. "We haven't made new friends in years! Do we even remember how to do it?"

It was true. After saying good-bye to my friends in Berkeley, I had flown to Boston to be with Ben. Since he'd already had a circle of friends, I had tried to just plug myself into his world. I'd chatted with his office mates at a Christmas party. I'd gotten coffee with a colleague of his who happened to have studied India. None of those casual friendships had evolved into anything more meaningful. Then we'd had Ella, which had made it hard to socialize at all. And even though I sometimes felt pangs of loneliness, making new friends seemed like a daunting task. I wasn't sure how to even start after moving again.

Friend making is a skill, and as we get older, we can get rusty at it. As children, our lives are structured to make socializing easy. People are neatly organized into groups based on their age and interests; we meet new kids at school, sports teams, debate prep, summer camp. When you participate in activities with the same people week after week, you discover commonalities and inside jokes. It's easy to go from being perfect strangers to being best friends. Then, these friends introduce you to new people, resulting in an ever-expanding network.

When we leave the organized social activities created by schools and parents, that built-in structure begins to disappear. To make things worse, sociologists have found that we fall into rigid routines that make it even harder to bump into new people. In our late twenties, we become increasingly prone to going back to the same grocery stores, taking the same routes to work, cooking with the same spices, and sitting at the same place at the dinner table.[30] In other words, we effectively optimize our lives to reduce the number of unknowns we encounter every day. This allows us not to waste valuable mental energy on things that aren't crucial, but it also cuts down on meeting new people. Interacting with strangers requires time, energy, and focus. We can't expect to just stumble into friendships as adults the way we did as children. We must go out of our way to make friends, leaving our comfort zone.

So what does this look like? Sociologists generally agree that there are three steps to creating a new friendship.[31] First, there is proximity: you need to be physically close to the potential friend, so you can interact with him or her face-to-face on a regular basis. Second, you need to have repeated—and importantly, *unplanned*—interactions with said person. And finally, you need to develop your nascent friendship in a setting where you can open up to each other emotionally. I decided to put this theory to the test. After all, I had nothing to lose. I was moving to Tallahassee. My nearest friend would be 1,300 miles away. I'd better befriend someone fast.

After the movers deposited our stuff in our new home, I laid out a plan that would effectively reverse engineer the friend-making process: First, I would identify a potential friend in close proximity, to facilitate optimal face-to-face contact. Second—and this seemed like the hardest step—I would have repeated and unplanned interactions with said target. And third, I would pull out the stops and open up to this person. How hard could it be?

Phase 1: Identify a Potential Friend in Close Proximity

Reality check: it's really hard. As I settle into Tallahassee, I realize that I don't actually have much in common with the people around me. When I introduce myself to people at my gym or fellow doughnut shop regulars, I always feel a bit let down. The average person in my new city has such a different sense of humor or political outlook that I can't see any common ground between us at all.

Then I meet Tara. I bump into her the first Sunday we attend a new church. I'm at the nursery, helping Ella settle in, but I'm dreading spending a full hour surrounded by drooling toddlers. I don't often get along with other parents of small children because they seem to want to talk only about the minutiae of their children's lives. ("Does your kid have a butt rash, too?") Maybe I'm a terrible mom, but I'd rather talk about where to go for a good cocktail.

Tara's different. She's on child care duty this week and couldn't be any more glamorous in skinny jeans, bright red lipstick, and chunky jewelry. As we begin talking, it turns out that although she is now a stay-at-home mom, she nearly pursued a PhD in English literature. She's curious about my doctoral work, which makes her one of the four people on the planet who are willing to listen to me prattle on about gender in ancient India. *This seems promising*, I think. Half an hour later, there we are, surrounded by screaming babies, chatting about our favorite philosophers.

Before I know it, the service is over, and just like that, so is our moment of bonding. We rush to our respective cars and dash home to put our kids down for their naps. I feel suddenly nostalgic for the days when I could meet someone I liked, then go out for drinks that night. But a few weeks later, I get a text on my phone from an unknown number. Hi Liz. It's Tara. Just wanted you to have my number in case you need anything as you settle down here in Tallahassee. XOXO.

My face lit up. Tara wanted to be my friend. I'd achieved phase one of the plan.

Phase 2: Have Regular, Unplanned Meetings

Then I ran into a big hurdle in friend making. Tara and I keep trying to do lunch. But one week I am struggling to finish a big project at work. Another week, her daughter gets sick and has to stay home from school. The simple act of coordinating our schedules threatens to torpedo our relationship before it even begins.

Suddenly the research all begins to make sense. Sociologists say that many friendships are formed when people can see each other in unplanned ways. In other words, meeting your new friend must be a pleasant side effect of doing something else you have already committed to do in your life, such as hiking a particular trail or going to the gym. Humans are extremely pragmatic when it comes to making friends. Early on, when you don't know someone well, it's unclear how much you want to invest in a new relationship. It takes some of the pressure off when you meet someone at an activity you've already made time for, such as yoga class or book club.

For Tara and me, this activity is church. We never actually get around to making plans to meet within the first few weeks of getting to know each other. But we keep bumping into each other on Sunday mornings, then at the church barbecue and the church Halloween party. We chat over pizza, laugh about funny Instagram memes we've seen, and generally realize that we still like each other. Our relationship evolves organically, in a relaxed way. We don't feel as much pressure to bond as we would if we were meeting over coffee. By the time we finally have brunch a few months into our friendship, we have so much to chat about.

Phase 3: Bond Emotionally

I'm making good progress. Now I just need to create the conditions for developing emotional intimacy.

I'm lucky. Tara, it turns out, is a pro at bonding. Me, not so much. It usually takes me a while to open up to people, but Tara gets right to it, which allows me to open up as well. The first time we have lunch, she is cheerful, funny, and engaging but doesn't shy away from talking honestly about her life. She brings up her complicated relationship with her mom, which lets me talk about my own struggles with my mother. We discuss how hard marriage can be sometimes and how weird it is to watch our bodies change during pregnancy.

"Mutual self-disclosure," as psychologists call it, is the glue that connects two people. To put it another way, if you want to deepen a friendship, you need to be vulnerable. In her research, Brené Brown has found that people who are capable of human connection are not scared to appear imperfect to other people. "They were willing to let go of who they thought they should be in order to be who they were," she said in a TEDx talk. " . . . You have to absolutely do that for connection."[32]

The problem is that if vulnerability was a muscle, it was one I hadn't used in a while. As Tara and I spent time together, I realized that opening up does not come easily to me. Even when I lived with Alan and Alex years ago, my tendency was to put on a brave, happy face so they would think I had my life together. But as time went on, I couldn't keep it up. They saw me go through breakups, lousy boyfriends, failed job searches, and many other disasters. More than that, I had to let them support me, which also made me uncomfortable, because I like to feel self-reliant.

Sociologists say that friendships deepen by giving and receiving help. This exchange allows two people to evolve from just enjoying each other's company to forging a bond of trust. My problem is that I like being the helpful friend, but I hate asking for help. When Alex had his eyes lasered, I was right there at the hospital to drive him home. When Alan got the flu, I went to the drugstore and picked up sixteen boxes of Theraflu. Meanwhile, it took years for me to graciously accept their support and help.

I was thinking about all of that one day in the winter, when I was on a business trip. Ben was at home in Tallahassee, and for the first time in thirty years, it snowed. After years of dealing with Boston's snowstorms, the light layer of snow on the ground seemed laughable to us. But Ella's day care closed for the day. And Ben couldn't spend the day at home with her because he had a meeting he couldn't cancel.

I texted Tara immediately to see if she knew of a babysitter who could stay with Ella. She responded that she'd be happy to take Ella for the day, since all of her kids would be home anyway. Tara was offering my family an easy solution to our little predicament, but I didn't want to say yes. It would be too much trouble, I thought. What if Ella needed a diaper change while she was there? With such a chaotic day ahead of her, I didn't want Tara having to wipe Ella's bottom, too.

After calling every babysitter we knew, we had no choice but to accept Tara's offer. So Ben dropped Ella off. Throughout the day, Tara texted sweet pictures of Ella playing at her house. In one picture, Ella is sitting at a cute little table along with Tara's own kids, eating a healthy lunch. It was a small gesture, but it had a deep impact on our relationship. I was eager to support her at any point down the line. And our relationship evolved from simply enjoying each other's company to being part of each other's support networks.

In many ways, the mission was complete. I had now made a friend, and she was wonderful. But then, like all good love stories, our relationship took a dramatic turn.

A year into our time in Florida, Ben got the job of his dreams at Harvard. It was back in Boston. That's right: the exact same town we had just moved from. I'll be frank, I kind of wanted to kill him. I had been so reluctant to move to Tallahassee in the first place, and as soon as we finally felt settled—and, more important, *I had made a friend*—he wanted to uproot us again. A lot of late nights ensued as we debated whether to stay or leave. But there was just no getting around it. Leaving was the best thing for our family. And my first thought, once we finally made the decision, was: How was I going to tell Tara?

I meet her at a local diner that serves the most enormous burgers I have ever seen. *We are going to deal with this by eating our feelings*, I think. I tell her the news, and as expected, her face crumples. She begins tearing up. We invested so much in this friendship, and it is about to be cut short. We order a jumbo banana split and eat it silently. After that day, we spend a few weeks texting each other about how sad we are. We try to spend as much time as we can with each other before the move. And we sit down with our calendars and plan for her to come up to Boston for a visit next May.

Our last few weeks in Florida, we go out for lunch every week, going to fancier and fancier restaurants, making the case to ourselves that it will be one of our last meals together in a long time. One week, we eat fried green tomatoes and coconut-crusted shrimp. The next week, we up the ante and go for truffle oil mac-and-cheese, followed by filet mignon.

Then it's my last week. We decide not to do a prolonged good-bye but instead give each other a quick hug and look forward to catching up in a few months. Two days later, I'm sitting in the Tallahassee airport alone with Ella, waiting to board our flight to Boston. Ben has gone ahead of us to set up the new house.

As we're waiting in front of our gate, Ella suddenly tells me she can't find her little stuffed elephant, Tilly. She left it at the Airbnb we slept in our last night in Tallahassee. She begins to sob. *Oh, crap,* I think. *Now I'm going to be stuck on a plane for five hours with an inconsolable toddler.*

I text Tara in a panic. And even though it's Saturday morning, she somehow kicks into high gear. She tells her two older children not to get into any trouble, grabs her youngest, and hops into her car. She tells me she'll go find Tilly and bring it to the airport. The clock's ticking. The flight leaves in forty-five minutes. "Tell security I'm coming," Tara texts me. So I go over to the security line and tell the TSA agents that Ella has left her stuffed elephant behind and it is absolutely imperative that our friend deliver it. Everyone is fully aware what a serious crisis this is, and they're all on alert.

Somehow Tara finds Tilly and brings her over. Ella and I are waiting behind the glass, past security, waiting to catch a glimpse of her. And then, just like that, Tara appears, carrying her daughter Sophie in one arm and Tilly in the other. Tara is beaming. The TSA agents—well-trained officers of the state—are fully prepared to execute. One agent takes Tilly, puts the elephant into a little crate, and sends it through the X-ray machine. They rush Tilly over to us. And I begin running to the plane with Ella in tow.

But not before taking one last look at Tara, throwing her kisses, waving good-bye.

SEVEN

POLITICS

When I was fifteen, my family moved to Jakarta, Indonesia, for my father's job at a time when the country was in the throes of political unrest. In 1998, the year before we arrived, tens of thousands of college students had taken to the streets to overthrow Suharto, the violent dictator who had been in power for thirty years. During his reign, Suharto had stolen $35 billion of taxpayer money and his armies had murdered up to a million people who had dared to defy his rule.[1] Young Indonesians were angry. Tens of thousands of them had gathered on the streets demanding change. They had occupied the Parliament building. And in the end, their voices had been heard. Suharto had resigned.

After we arrived in our new city and settled into daily life, I watched that activism continue to play out. Throughout high school, I saw young people in front of government buildings calling for free elections and economic policies that would create jobs.

The summer before college, I got a chance to see the protests up close. A family friend, John Aglionby, was a journalist covering the demonstrations in the city and invited me to tag along. I met him in a park downtown. He handed me a press pass to wear around my neck, and together we set out into the crowds. I remember feeling a strange kind of electricity in the air. In the background, stereos were blasting punk music and people were beating on makeshift drums. Every so often, you could hear protestors chanting *"Reformasi!"* which meant "Reform!" It felt a little like a carnival, except that there were military guards stationed on the outer ridges of the square and massive tanks sat on street corners.

The protestors were mostly college students just a few years older than I was at the time. They wore bandanas, jeans, and T-shirts covered with the logos of heavy-metal bands. I marveled at how sure they were about what they were fighting for. As John interviewed them, they talked about their vision of a government free of corruption and a thriving middle class. They were chanting because they believed their voices mattered. And they were right. Through their protests, they changed the fate of their country, which had a ripple effect throughout Southeast Asia. Through their protests, they effectively changed the world.

I was in awe of those youth activists but also a little unnerved by them. At eighteen, I had absolutely no idea what I stood for politically. When I came to the United States for college, I could not think of an issue I cared enough about to take to the streets at the risk of being sprayed by tear gas. Hell, I barely understood how voting worked. As a result, I struggled to find my political voice in my twenties. I wasn't alone. As we'll see, data show that most twentysomethings aren't politically active.

We've all heard inspiring stories of youth revolutions here in the United States, from the civil rights movement to the Vietnam War protests. But the truth is, it can be very hard for the average twentysomething to participate in the political process. Everything about politics, especially voting, is wrapped up in layers of bureaucracy. It requires specialized knowledge and skills to participate, and most of us are never taught how to get started. And then there's the fact that today's twenty-somethings have good reasons to feel particularly disillusioned with the government. The generations that came before us accumulated massive debts that will likely eat into our own Medicare and Social Security. And they did nothing to stop college tuition from ballooning to the point that most of us are drowning in debt. It's hard to care about the government when you feel as though the government does not care about you.

At the same time, many young people care deeply about what is happening in the world around them; they're just struggling to figure out what to do about it. Surveys show that compared to older Americans, younger ones are much more concerned about tackling climate change[2] and racism.[3] They are much more likely to support giving immigrants a pathway to citizenship.[4] So the question is how to harness all of this passion and turn it into real change.

I recently interviewed DeRay Mckesson onstage at the annual Fair Trade Campaigns National Conference, which brings together thousands of college students who care about workers' rights around the world. In his late twenties, DeRay spent every weekend and holiday driving twelve hours from his hometown of Baltimore to Ferguson, Missouri, to join the Black Lives Matter protestors. He eventually quit his job as a public school teacher to devote himself entirely to the movement and has become one of the best-known civil rights activists of our time.

At the conference, one student in the audience asked him how to get more involved in politics. DeRay's answer was interesting.

He didn't start by talking about registering to vote or getting a crash course in political organizing, although these are things he actively supports. If you force yourself to get more involved in politics just because you think it is the right thing to do, DeRay says, it will feel like work, and you'll be unlikely to stick with it long term. Instead, he thinks twentysomethings should pay attention to what problems in the world break their hearts or rile them up, then bring their energy into the political fight. "You should follow your own curiosity," he says. "When some issue in politics or civic life captures your attention, learn as much as you can about it and then find ways to contribute to the cause right where you are, in your own community."

Everyone will have a slightly different jumping-off point when it comes to politics, based on the different political beliefs, interests, and causes that animate him or her. But figuring out how to contribute to causes you care about matters because the policies that come out of the political process shape our everyday reality, from how much college debt we accrue to whether police feel empowered to brutalize people of color. It's never too late to start advocating for policies that will change the country both now and in the decades to come.

WHY POLITICS IS IMPORTANT IN YOUR TWENTIES

Over the last few years, student movements similar to what I witnessed in Indonesia have sprung up here in the United States. In 2013, three women in their late twenties launched Black Lives Matter, drawing worldwide attention to systemic racism and violence toward African Americans. After the Parkland shooting in 2018, high schoolers organized the March for Our Lives, which spurred nearly two million people around the world to take to the streets, demanding stronger gun control legislation. In the 2018 midterm elections, Alexandria Ocasio-Cortez became the youngest woman ever to be elected to Congress at twenty-nine. She became the face of the Green New Deal, a dramatic proposal to combat climate change in the United States.

Reading the headlines, it would seem as though millennials and Gen Zers are very politically active. But the reality is that these young activists are actually the exception to the rule. The majority of American twentysomethings aren't participating in the political process. Let's take voting, for example. Millennials are quickly becoming the largest generation in the country and also the largest voting bloc.[5] But they're not using their political power fully. In the 2016 presidential election, only 46 percent of those under the age of thirty voted,[6] and in the 2018 midterms, that figure went down to 35.6 percent.[7] That was significantly lower than for those sixty-five and older, who turned out at rates of 72 percent and 66.1 percent, respectively. That's why the polling stations are a sea of silver hair and walking canes.

Since millennials and Gen Zers do not have a strong voice in the political process, the older generations are the ones who are actively shaping the country's future. And the problem is that they want totally different things from us.

Older voters tend to be wealthier and more conservative than young ones, and their political choices reflect that, from banning abortion six weeks after conception to keeping the minimum wage as low as $7.25 in some states. Many policies that older voters are pushing for will negatively affect our entire lives: the over-sixty-five crowd has not been invested in fighting climate change, putting away funds for future generations, or making college affordable so students today aren't saddled with mountains of debt. As young people, we have more life ahead of us, which means we will be wrestling with the consequences of these decisions long after the people who made them are gone.

Many surveys show that young Americans do not like where the country is going. Pew Research Center found that around 70 percent of millennials and Gen Zers disapproved of the Trump presidency, which is far higher than among older generations.[8] Millennials are also among the most left-leaning generations. Seventy percent of them believe that the government should do more to solve social problems; 62 percent also think that increasing racial and ethnic diversity is good for society. In terms of party affiliation, 54 percent of millennials identify as Democrats, 39 percent as Republicans, and 11 percent as independents.[9] And young Republicans tend to have more progressive views on social issues such as race, gender, and sexual orientation than older Republicans do.

Given our political preferences, it makes sense that the election of Donald Trump sparked outrage among our generation. But part of the reason Trump was elected in the first place is that we did not show up at the polls in 2016. A recent Pew survey about the 2016 presidential election asked respondents a series of questions about their demographics and voting preferences, then independently verified whether they had voted or not. When you crunch the numbers, the results show that if people under the age of thirty who didn't vote had come out to the polls, they would have shifted the votes for Clinton by slightly under one percentage point, equivalent to more than a million votes. In the context of the 2016 election, which was very close, that might well have changed the outcome.[10]

There's also another reason why politics is important in your twenties. As with many other behaviors we've seen in this book, what you do early on in life has a way of tending to stick with you. As we saw in the fitness and hobby chapters, our rocket years are the time when we form habits. The political decisions you make early on—whether to vote, which party to affiliate with, what causes you donate to, whether you get involved with advocacy groups—are likely to be lasting ones.

Political scientists have known for a long time that people who develop habits of civic engagement early on tend to stay politically engaged throughout their lives, setting them on a different trajectory than their peers. One researcher asked high school seniors about their interest in politics, then tracked them eight, seventeen, and thirty-two years later.[11] Roughly half of the respondents had exactly the same level of political interest throughout that time. Party affiliation also tends to stay very consistent over time. People's choice of political party is similar, in many ways, to a religious affiliation: it takes a lot to change it.[12] When people do change their political party, they tend to do so slowly and because they have noticed that others in the communities they belong to (such as their colleagues at work and neighbors) have started to drift toward another party.[13] So your initial political choices matter.

Voting seems to follow a similar pattern. Once you've voted in a couple of presidential and midterm elections, it becomes a habit. One study found that voters who turned eighteen just in time to vote in an election were roughly five percentage points more likely to vote four years later than those who had narrowly missed the age cutoff in the earlier election.[14] In other words, having voted just once made a sizable difference the next time around.

Even protesting appears to be a learned behavior. People who have been to just one protest are more inclined to attend another one. Take the example of the protests in Hong Kong that sprang up in 2019. Researchers paid some students at a

Hong Kong university to gather information about a protest that was occurring. Some were randomly assigned to attend the protest, and others were assigned to collect data without actually attending. Surprisingly, the students who attended the protest were more likely to attend future protests as well, even without a financial incentive.[15] It's clear that getting politically involved will help you shape the decisions that will affect the rest of your life, and developing political habits early will make it more likely that you'll continue to stay active.

WHY IS IT SO HARD FOR TWENTYSOMETHINGS TO GET INVOLVED?

There are two reasons for the gap in political activity between twentysomethings and older people. First of all, every generation tends to grow more politically involved as it ages. This is a well-known reality in political science. When you look at the percentage of each age group that turns out to vote in elections, it seems to go up as people get older, peaking when they are in their midsixties, then declining.

But second, it's important to note that although twentysomethings have always been less inclined to vote than older folks, millennials and Gen Zers are facing even more economic and political hurdles to getting involved in politics than their parents or grandparents did.

We're not the first generation of young people to vote in low numbers. In the United States, it wasn't so long ago that people under the age of twenty-one were not even considered old enough to vote. It was only during the 1960s, when eighteen-year-olds were drafted to fight in the Vietnam War, that activists made the case that there was something wrong with sending young men off to die but not giving them the right to vote. All of that lobbying worked, and in 1972 the voting age was lowered to eighteen through ratification of the Twenty-sixth Amendment.

But when eighteen-year-olds finally gained the right to vote, they did not exactly beat down the door to get to the polling booths. The 1972 election, which pitted Richard Nixon against George McGovern, presented a stark choice for the direction of the country. McGovern ran on a platform to end the war in Vietnam immediately, in contrast to Nixon, who wanted to keep troops in the country. Nonetheless, only half of eligible eighteen- to twenty-four-year-olds turned out to vote; on the other hand, 70 percent of those aged twenty-five and older turned out.[16] You know what happened next: Nixon won.

That wasn't an isolated scenario. In the last four decades, young people have continued to vote in lower numbers than older citizens. In 2012, for instance, there was still a turnout gap of almost 25 percentage points between individuals in the eighteen-to-twenty-four age range and their older counterparts.[17] The gaps in turnout are even greater when comparing people aged eighteen to twenty-four with folks in their sixties; depending on the election, the age turnout gap can be 35 percentage points or more.[18]

Political scientists have found that it takes time to learn the ropes when it comes to politics. As people settle into their adult lives, they have more time to learn about the political issues that will affect them, helping them understand what is at stake in elections. As people get older, they are more likely to follow politics in the news and understand basic facts about the political parties.[19] Over time, people seem to get better at jumping through bureaucratic hoops, such as figuring out how to register and finding their polling place.

But that's not all. Political scientists believe that as people get older, they experience life events that make them more invested in politics. They put down roots in a community, get full-time jobs, buy a home, have children, and develop health conditions, all of which make them more interested in policies such as taxes, the school system, and health care. When you're paying thousands of dollars a year on property taxes, you're going to make damn sure your city department of public works fixes the pothole on your street.

I was lucky to have Ben, my own personal political scientist, to explore this in more depth. He downloaded data from the Current Population Survey, which has asked people about voting and other aspects of their lives for more than two decades.[20] Analyzing the data provides clues about what might make twenty-somethings more or less likely to vote. He found that being married appears to have no impact on whether someone votes. Interestingly, living with one's parents appears to produce a slight uptick in turnout, revealing that parents might nudge their adult children who live at home to vote. On the other hand, graduating from college, owning a home, being employed, and being in the top third income bracket all clearly make young people more likely to vote. In other words, financial stability seems to play a big role in motivating people to participate politically.

This makes intuitive sense. Having more money makes people care more about the economy and how their taxes are spent, which are two of the most obvious ways that politics affects our lives. But millennials came of age during the Great Recession, which has made it harder for them to find jobs and pay off debt than the generations that came before. Those under thirty-five are suffering through the biggest wealth gap between younger and older Americans on record. That's why some people refer to millennials as "Generation Screwed."[21]

MILLENNIALS GOT A RAW DEAL

Millennials, as well as Gen Zers, are dealing with economic conditions that make it more difficult for them to get involved in politics. Young people are finding it harder and harder to achieve financial independence, thanks to things such as crippling student debt and low wages, and this makes it harder to reach a stage of life where they can invest in their community.

Millennials' experience provides a good case study of how financial setbacks can negatively impact young people's political participation. The share of twentysomething homeowners was rising until 2006, but after the beginning of the financial crisis, it began falling. The share of people in their twenties living with their parents began increasing steadily at around the time of the financial crisis as well. In 1996, fewer than 30 percent of people in their twenties lived at home with their parents or other relatives; by 2016, that number was closer to 35 percent. The most important change was the increase in unemployment among twentysomethings that coincided with the financial crisis. The unemployment rate for people in their twenties went from a low of 5 percent in 2000 to a peak of almost 12 percent in 2010.

Ben estimated that the overall impact of the crisis drove millennials to vote at a rate 5 percentage points lower than they would have if the recession had not happened. To figure that out, he created a model that took into account a wide range of factors that influenced millennial voting behavior. He found that twentysomethings had not felt the full effects of the crisis right as it occurred but in the years that followed from 2009 onward. For instance, it took a while for companies to reduce the number of entry-level workers they hired and to cut their internship programs in response to the recession. The negative effects of the recession played out over several years after the height of the crisis.

When he looked at the entire data set, he found that there were actually some aspects of the recession that made young people *more* likely to vote. For instance, many millennials had chosen to ride out the economic crisis by pursuing higher education and living at home, both of which tend to increase voting behavior slightly, as we just saw. But those small increases in political participation were obliterated by the financial hurdles that millennials experienced. Relative to the rest of the population, twentysomethings experienced greater unemployment as a result of the financial crisis. They were 5 percent less likely to own a home. The recession also led millennials to move more frequently, thanks to losing a job or having their home foreclosed. Moving leads to a decrease in voting because it takes time to get a new driver's license and register to vote in your new state.

This case study focuses on millennials during and right after the recession. But the lessons apply to twentysomethings more broadly. As young people increasingly cannot support themselves with entry-level jobs, we can extrapolate using these results to predict that all of the obstacles to achieving various life goals (buying a house, getting married, and so on) will continue to depress young people's involvement in politics.

There are legitimate reasons young Americans aren't participating in politics. But by not taking a bigger role in the nation's decision making, we're also not advocating for policies that could help us get out of our financial rut and thrive in the years to come. It's a vicious cycle.

Our best way forward is to take back our political power. We can support a new generation of political candidates who are fighting for positions that will benefit us. We can work to make sure that officials who are already in power know that they need to pay more attention to our needs. There are many ways for us to get more involved in the political process and even help others in our generation to take part. It will take a systematic and concerted effort, but it is well within our reach. So how can we get started?

HOW TO TAKE BACK OUR POLITICAL POWER

I became a US citizen at the age of thirty-two. The first time I had the right to vote in the country was during the 2016 election, and, for me, the stakes could not have been any higher. Throughout that year, Ben and I watched the political drama unfold during the primaries. On the Democratic side, Hillary Clinton and Bernie Sanders were laying out different visions for America. On the Republican side, there was a crowded field of presidential hopefuls, including a surprising candidate with no previous government experience, Donald Trump.

I was thrilled to make my voice heard in that historic election, but then I realized that there was a mountain of paperwork to do before I could even get started. And on top of that, I learned that I wasn't just responsible for picking a president; I also had to learn about all the local propositions and down-ballot races. I felt overwhelmed. On several occasions, while trying to figure out the nuances of a local bill about charter schools, I felt like giving up altogether. I cared a lot about what was happening in the country, yet I couldn't figure out how to act on my beliefs. I also felt silly not knowing the basics of the political process in my early thirties. I assumed that everybody else my age had figured out how to vote more than a decade before. But as we've seen in this chapter, that's just not true.

Most people in the United States don't learn how to vote or participate in the political process in school, so it falls on the individual to figure all of this out in the late teens and early twenties. As a result, researchers have found, twentysomethings don't understand the basics about voting in elections, registering to vote, or contacting their elected officials. The younger you are when you develop these skills, the easier it will be for you to become a more active citizen. So the most valuable thing you can do in your rocket years is get a handle on how to do these things.

One option is to take advantage of websites such as TurboVote, an online service that helps you figure out how to register to vote online and notifies you of upcoming elections. It can be particularly useful for navigating complications such as figuring out how to vote by mail if you are a student whose residence is in another state. I've also found that figuring out how to vote is made easier by talking to people who have done it and who understand the process well. In my case, I talked to Ben, who obviously knew a lot about it because it is his area of expertise. If you happen to have close friends or family members who are politically active, they're a great place to start. You should feel free to ask them questions that you think are embarrassingly elementary because the truth is that nothing about the political system is simple. Your friends also had to figure these things out at one point, and they will very likely empathize with your confusion.

I also talked to my neighbors about where our polling place was and what to expect when I got there. I started paying attention to local news, rather than just the national, so I could figure out who was running in down-ballot races and what the local issues in my district were. And over time, I found that the more I learned about how the process worked and my own place in it, the more interested in it I became. I started to care more about the politics section in the newspaper. I had much more to talk about with my politically minded friends; together, we'd weigh the pros and cons of different bills.

It wasn't long before I was interested in taking my political involvement up a notch. If you're at that point, too, there are lots of different ways to do so, but here, we'll focus on two of the most straightforward ones: getting other young people to turn out to vote and participating in peaceful protests against policies that you disagree with. In each of these areas, there is a bundle of useful social science research that provides some helpful tips about what works and what doesn't.

Help Get Out the Vote

If you want to make a difference in politics, one of the best things you can do is to join an organization that will help you advocate for something you care about by engaging with other people around you. Research shows that efforts to mobilize others can make a real difference. Though I relied largely on friends and family to help me learn about politics, there are actually many organizations out there specifically devoted to educating people about the basics of voting. These are called get-out-the-vote (GOTV) efforts. They're organized either by neutral political organizations, such as Rock the Vote and FairVote, or by a particular political candidate who stands to do well in an election by encouraging people to vote in neighborhoods where most people support his or her candidacy. Barack Obama, for example, had a massive GOTV operation.

Political scientists have studied the effectiveness of door-to-door canvassing and have found that it consistently drives real results, increasing the odds that someone contacted will vote.

In one landmark study, researchers ran an experiment in which they contacted randomly selected voters in New Haven, Connecticut, then tracked whether those contacted had been more likely to vote in an election than residents who had not been contacted.[22] Direct person-to-person contact by a canvasser raised the turnout rate by almost ten percentage points for those contacted versus those not contacted. It was much more effective than other, less personal forms of contact. Receiving mailings, for instance, raised the turnout rate only slightly—by about one-half of a percentage point—and receiving a phone call did not have any effect. If you can help provide that personal touch—whether canvassing for a political campaign or collecting signatures for a cause—the evidence shows that it is rarely a wasted effort.

A follow-up study by some of the same researchers showed that applying peer pressure worked surprisingly well.[23] The researchers sent out a mailing that revealed whether or not your neighbors had voted and stated that after the election, neighbors would receive a similar mailer informing them of whether or not you had cast a ballot. Residents who received the mailing about their neighbor's voting habits were about eight percentage points more likely to turn out than those who received no contact. You could easily work this insight into your own interactions. Let your family and friends know that you plan to vote, and ask them their plans.

There is evidence that campaigns are not doing everything they can to target twentysomethings, largely because they find young people harder to reach than older folks. When one researcher, David Nickerson, examined six GOTV efforts around the country, he found that young people were just as easy to convince to vote as older people. However, actually getting in touch with young people was significantly harder, partly because they were less likely to have a stable, permanent address.[24] This makes sense: college or graduate students often move on a yearly basis. And even when canvassers have the right address, twentysomethings are less likely to be at home. On an average evening, they might be studying at the library or spending the evening at their significant other's house.

Many GOTV organizations figure that since it is hard—and expensive—to reach young people, they should just give up and target their older peers. But this seems like faulty logic to me. Millennials will soon be the largest voting bloc, so it makes sense to do everything possible to figure out how to reach them now. If traditional methods such as going door to door don't work for young people, perhaps it's time to ramp up new approaches, such as organizing block parties or pop-up events.

This isn't just true of GOTV efforts. Campaigns and political organizations across the board believe that reaching young people is harder and more expensive.[25] Any help we can provide, both for political causes (such as pro- or antigun groups, pro- or antiabortion groups, and so on) and for election campaigns, can make a particularly big difference because outreach efforts typically don't focus on younger folks.

You can help in these efforts. The bottom line is that twentysomethings can be nudged to be more politically engaged. We just need to keep working to meet them where they are. And once someone becomes a voter, evidence suggests that he or she will be more likely to continue voting in the years to come.

Protest

Elections don't occur that often. Sometimes you just can't wait, and you need to take immediate political action. This is where protesting comes into play. Publicly assembling with other people and peacefully speaking out for change is another effective form of political action. We've seen protest movements work in the past, including in the areas of women's suffrage and civil rights. But we're also in a moment of great protest right now, with Black Lives Matter, the Women's March, March for Our Lives, and the Global Climate Strike. Mass political protests have been shown to lead to meaningful policy change both directly and indirectly. If you're interested in participating in or even helping to organize a protest for an issue you care about, there are some key lessons to cull from research on what leads people to show up for protests.

First, protestors care about how many other people will show up at a protest. In situations in which there is real risk of a crackdown on protestors—for example, as in the case of the protestors in Hong Kong—then informing a potential attendee that a lot of other people are planning to attend can actually depress turnout, since large protests are more likely to be shut down by the government.[26] On the other hand, in contexts where there is little risk for the protestors and a show of widespread support is likely to matter in seeking policy concessions (think, for example, of the March for Our Lives seeking legislation to prevent future gun violence), helping potential protestors understand that it will be a large-scale event will make them more likely to participate.

In the United States, the Constitution enshrines the right to assemble peaceably. There have been times when nonviolent protest has been met with repression, such as during the civil rights movement, but compared to authoritarian states, the United States has a better track record of allowing peaceful protests to proceed. As a result, if you are organizing an event in the United States, your protest is not likely to be at risk of a crackdown. Organizing a successful event will hinge on getting a critical mass of people to commit and then communicating to new people that others are actually going to show up.

One effective way to do that is to make it clear that protestors will receive recognition for participating. Protesting is inherently a social behavior, one that helps people signal their political positions to the world. It turns out that people are more likely to show up to a protest if they know their actions are likely to be broadcast to other people.

In one recent study, a political scientist partnered with an LGBTQ organization and ran an experiment testing the effectiveness of different types of appeals to participate in a protest that was recognizing the repeal of "Don't ask, don't tell" in the military and supporting marriage equality. The researcher sent out various types of invitations to the event: one with just the basics, one noting that participants would be recognized in a monthly newsletter, and one inviting participants to post photos from the protest on the Facebook page of the organization. Receiving a message emphasizing recognition for attendance led more people to commit to attending and then to actually follow through. People who received such messages were about fifteen percentage points more likely to show up than those who were sent just the basic details about the event, most likely because it meant being recognized by other people who cared about the same cause.[27] In other words, if you can create opportunities to broadcast a protest, such as posting videos or photos on social media, people are more likely to attend. Doing this can boost the likelihood that protestors will attend and will help give voice to whatever issue you are advocating for.

When I think about why to get involved in politics, I keep coming back to DeRay Mckesson's advice. He says that getting engaged in the political process often starts small. A particular social injustice, such as homelessness in your neighborhood or the gender wage gap, might catch your attention. You can choose to do nothing about it, or, as DeRay suggests, you can try to learn more about the issue in the way that feels most authentic to you. If you're naturally extroverted, you might participate in door-to-door canvassing to encourage people to vote on a resolution that will tackle the problem. If you're introverted, on the other hand, you might be more comfortable writing to your elected official. Political involvement should feel meaningful and empowering, never a burden.

In the summer of 2018, when we were living in Tallahassee for the year, Ben and I took Ella to her first protest. She was two and a half. We had spent the previous few weeks horrified at the news that the Trump administration was cracking down on illegal immigration by separating children of immigrants from their parents at the border. On a Saturday afternoon, the three of us stood in front of the Florida State Capitol along with several hundred other people to voice our opposition to that cruel and inhumane policy.

As we pushed Ella in her stroller, she wanted to know what exactly we were up to. We didn't know what to tell her. It seemed wrong to scare her with details about children her age who were being yanked from their parents' arms and incarcerated in converted Walmart buildings. But Ben, who is a political scientist after all, thought it was never too soon to introduce our daughter to the basics of civic engagement. He tried to explain the concept of a protest in simple terms. "When your leaders do something you don't think is good, you can tell them, 'I don't like this. It's not right,'" he told her.

It's unclear whether Ella got very much out of that lesson, but she did think her father looked pretty funny wagging his finger in the air. For a two-year-old, the demonstration seemed like a bundle of laughs. Bands came up to a podium to perform songs about justice and families. Ella danced and clapped along. Every so often, the crowd would chant, "Families belong together." Ella would try to join in. Some people had scribbled slogans on colorful posterboard. Others were handing out snacks and bottled water, to help us survive the Florida heat. Ella was thrilled to receive a small packet of goldfish crackers.

Unlike at the demonstration in Jakarta, there were no tanks on street corners or menacing security forces patrolling the event. There was one policeman wandering about, but he seemed fairly jovial. He gave Ella a high five before turning his attention to helping an old lady who looked tired. I felt grateful to have the right to protest. We felt safe on those steps, voicing our objection to what the government was doing. And in the end, we saw democracy playing out as it should. All of that public pressure prompted Trump to sign an executive order ending family separations, although there would be a long way to go to reunite children with their parents.

I am trying to make up for lost time. I am glad that Ella will not have as steep a learning curve as I did. She'll probably tag along at other protests and go with us to polling stations when she's older. The idea of being involved in the political process won't seem so intimidating to her. And hopefully she won't wait till she's thirty-two to vote for the first time.

EIGHT

FAITH

I've always loved hearing how my parents met. As a child, I asked them to tell the tale so many times that it has taken on a mythic quality in my mind. It is, after all, my origin story. It goes like this.

The year was 1960. In a small town in Malaysia, there was a little Baptist church. My mother, a five-year-old with round cheeks, noticed my father, a skinny six-year-old, visiting her Sunday school class. My father liked to say that my mother made eyes at him, because even at that age, he was irresistible. At the time, it was improbable that a Chinese girl and an Indian boy, barely out of toddlerhood, would become friends and grow up together, but there they were, sneaking glances at each other on the church pews. It wasn't until they both left home that they started dating. My father moved to the nation's capital, Kuala Lumpur, to attend university, while my mother went off to nursing school on Penang Island. They wrote letters to each other and saved up money to take the bus and train to see each other when they could. In their early twenties, they decided to get married.

When I think about my family's beginnings, it occurs to me that it is an accident of history that I come from a Christian family. My father came from a long line of devout Tamil-speaking Hindus. His home was filled with shrines to Ganesha, the elephant-headed god of wisdom. The whole church thing was really my grandmother's idea. She had gotten it into her head that her sons needed to improve their English so they could do well in school. What better way to do so than to expose them to the American missionaries who often visited the local church?

The plan worked a little too well. My father and his three brothers ended up with an impeccable command of the English language, which helped them thrive in school and their eventual careers. What my grandmother could not have foreseen was that each of her sons would also develop a profound and enduring Christian faith. When my father and uncles entered their rocket years, it was the Christian framework they relied on to figure out their values and purpose in the world. And then, when they had families of their own, they deepened their involvement with the church. That is why, as a preschooler, I spent Sunday mornings rearranging the plastic animals in a Noah's ark toy set at the church nursery and dutifully practicing my nonspeaking role as a sheep in the Christmas play. One of my earliest memories is of saying bedtime prayers with my parents, certain that some sort of cosmic being cared about the minutiae of my life.

As I grew up, I found that the everyday religious practices that I had learned as a child, such as praying and meditating, were useful, because they gave me the space to nurture an inner life. At services on Sunday, I sometimes felt moments of transcendence, when I felt connected to a force bigger than myself. And as I went through my rocket years, my faith equipped me to survive the most difficult moment of my life. When I was twenty-eight, my father died unexpectedly from complications during heart surgery. He was only fifty-five. As you have probably gathered from this book, my father had been the most important person in my universe. He had been my best friend and the wisest, kindest person I knew. I fell into a bottomless hole of grief. For two years, I withdrew from the world and turned inward. But as I burrowed deep inside myself, I found something powerful there that pointed me to the possibility that there is more to this life than we can see in the physical world. And ultimately, one reason I decided to hold onto my faith was that I wanted to be able to access that mysterious well of strength in the years to come.

I tell this story, as specific as it is, because everybody's belief system is deeply personal and idiosyncratic, shaped by our family history, life experiences, and personality. Yet our ideology, whether religious or secular, plays an important role in our rocket years by helping us identify our values and priorities as we chart the course for our lives. The spiritual paths we take in our twenties can also shape our lives in profound ways that may not be obvious for years. Our religious identity will influence the kinds of communities we will be part of throughout our lives and the beliefs we will instill in our children. For me, faith provides a framework for thinking about existential issues that are rarely addressed in other areas of life. Most world religions have philosophies about the meaning of life, what it means to have a soul, and what happens after death. These ideas can shape how we cope with the periods of hardship and trauma that will inevitably come our way.

In these pages, I consider how your relationship to your childhood religion changes when you move away from home, confront ideas that challenge your beliefs, and start a family.

Increasingly, millennials and Gen Zers leave organized religion because they don't support the political stances their denominations have taken. Some of these young people say they miss the community and traditions that they enjoyed when they were growing up, so I also consider what it takes to stay connected to a vibrant, meaningful, intergenerational community outside traditional religious institutions.

THE GREAT EXODUS FROM ORGANIZED RELIGION

My decision to stick with religion goes against the grain for my generation. Today's young people are opting out of organized religion in droves, driving a broader cultural change in the United States and transforming it into a more secular society.[1] As millennials rewrite the rules about religion, houses of worship are emptying out. I've observed this myself. When Ben and I visit a church, it's a sea of silver heads. We're often the youngest people in the congregation. Many don't have a nursery for Ella because children haven't been seen in the pews in years.

Sociologists, including those at Pew Research Center and the Public Religion Research Institute (PRRI), are fascinated by religious trends because they offer insight into how society operates, from where people make friends to how they vote. When I first looked into this data, I was surprised by how young people are when they commit to the religious beliefs—including atheism or agnosticism—that will carry them through their lives. I always assumed that people began to ponder deep, existential questions as they got older and closer to the end of their own lives, but research shows that people don't generally switch religions after the age of thirty.[2] Sixty-two percent of people who have left organized religion altogether did so before they turned eighteen, and 28 percent say they did so between the ages of eighteen and twenty-nine.[3]

Our rocket years are a prime time to question the religious teachings of our childhood. In 1981, James Fowler, a theological scholar, came up with a psychological model that lays out the six stages of faith that humans experience and is still used by researchers today. The model begins in preschool, when we are likely to confuse fantasy with reality, and ends in old age, when we begin to accept the strange, mystical paradoxes in life. Fowler found that the twenties are particularly turbulent because many people begin to question whether they ever truly believed the religious beliefs they were raised with.[4] This is partly because we are suddenly exposed to alternative spiritual paths as we meet new people, travel to new places, or learn about other religions in college. Millennials have even more access to other cultures and beliefs than previous generations did; they grew up with the internet at their fingertips and low-cost airlines tickets at their disposal, making it easier for them to learn about new ideas and cultures that might challenge their beliefs.

An increasing number of millennials and Gen Zers are no longer interested in being associated with their childhood religion—or any organized religion at all. According to the PRRI, 39 percent of people aged between eighteen and twenty-nine describe themselves as religiously unaffiliated. (Sociologists sometimes describe these people as "nones" because they do not check off any religious denomination in surveys.)[5] Only 9 percent of Americans grew up in a nonreligious household, so most of these now-unaffiliated people grew up with a religious identity. For comparison, only 10 percent of young adults identified themselves as religiously unaffiliated back in the 1980s. In its 2014 landmark survey of religion in America, Pew found that only 27 percent of twentysomethings attended religious services on a weekly basis, compared to 38 percent of people in their fifties and 51 percent of people in their seventies and older.[6] Given what we know about how religious identities don't change much after the rocket years, it is unlikely that these "nones" will show up at church or temple in the years to come.

This represents an unprecedented cultural shift, one that researchers are still trying to understand. When you parse through studies, you see that young people report many reasons for choosing not to identify with any religion. Pew surveys have found that 60 percent of "nones" left their childhood religion because they no longer believe its teachings.[7] The second most common reason, cited by 49 percent of respondents, is that they don't like the social and political positions taken by churches. A PRRI survey found that 29 percent of "nones" had been influenced by hearing negative teachings about or seeing negative treatment of LGBTQ people.[8] In other words, there are many twentysomethings who haven't given up on the notion of God, but they don't want to be part of churches, temples, or mosques that don't reflect their values.

Some sociologists see millennials' rejection of religion as part of their broader lack of trust in institutions of all kinds, from the government to marriage to the labor market, which failed them when they needed a job in the postrecession years.[9] Across all denominations, Catholics have suffered the largest decline among major religious groups: 13 percent of Americans are now former Catholics.[10] One theory for this sharp decline is that Catholicism is the most institutional of the Christian denominations, full of rigid hierarchies and a centralized power structure based in the Vatican, which governs Catholic churches around the world.

One piece of data that supports this theory is that other religious groups, especially those that are organized in a more decentralized way, have lost fewer millennials. Minorities, in particular, are more likely to be part of thriving spiritual communities, partly because these religious groups tend to be very grassroots. Black churches have seen relatively little attrition among young people, and black millennials are considerably more religious than others in their generation, with 64 percent reporting that they are highly religious.[11] And among people who grew up as Hindus, Muslims, or Jews, more than three-quarters continue to identify with their childhood faiths. One reason for this may be that religious leaders in these faiths tend to be embedded in their communities and better able to address the needs of the people who show up week after week. For minorities, places of worship play an important functional role within the community as well, providing an important place to gather, share resources, and support one another.

The twentysomethings who leave organized religion may be losing out on some of these social bonds. Some sociologists worry about what will happen to American society if these faith-based communities disintegrate. Until recently, religion served as a way to bring people together. The church, synagogue, or temple offered a safe space for people to make friends and find help in times of need. In the past, people often found their romantic partners in church because it was easier to find someone who shared your values. (That was certainly my parents' story; as a mixed-race couple, they did not share a similar culture, but being at church together highlighted their shared beliefs.) Faith-based groups often carried people through life, helping them commemorate births, marriages, and deaths.

Several large studies have shown that people who attend religious services tend to experience less psychological distress and have higher levels of personal well-being.[12] Psychologists say that this might have nothing to do with faith at all but simply the fact that religion is inherently community oriented. Not attending church might simply mean less interpersonal contact overall. This is troubling, as I noted in the friendship chapter, because doctors have found that weak social connections can have negative health effects. As we've seen, millennials and Gen Zers feel lonelier than older generations do. And feeling isolated lowers a person's life span, carrying the same mortality risk as smoking fifteen cigarettes a day.[13]

The solution isn't for young people to jump back into churches, temples, mosques, and synagogues even if they don't believe what is being preached from the pulpit. In interviews with "nones," researchers have found that people generally feel good about their decision to leave a religion whose teachings or positions they find offensive. But some of them say they do miss the relationships that religion fosters. In surveys, these people talk about how much they enjoyed singing in the choir or making friends from other generations. If this is how you feel, it might be worth trying to find other forms of community that are more authentic to you. The good news is that twenty-somethings are actively creating communities that better reflect their values and approach to spirituality.

MILLENNIALS ARE REINVENTING RELIGION

Many religiously unaffiliated young people don't have any desire for a community that resembles church. They would rather pour what little free time they have into other activities that give them purpose, such as spending time with their family and friends or doing their hobbies. Thirty-seven percent of people who do not attend religious services regularly say they practice their faith in other ways, which could mean anything from pushing their body to its limits to pursuing a career that helps make the world a better place.[14] Many companies are trying to fill this void. Brands that target millennials say they want to create a community among their customers and hire "community managers" for this task. Coworking spaces such as WeWork and the Wing advertise themselves as places where you can connect with people who share your values and interests. Media brands such as theSkimm have private Facebook groups and in-person events where readers can meet one another. Fitness clubs such as SoulCycle and CrossFit encourage members to bond over their shared workouts.

But for some, this kind of corporate community is not enough. There are some people who have stopped believing in God but miss many of the unique things that churches offered, such as singing together or studying a sacred text. This has given rise to a new movement to create alternative churches. Take, for instance, the rise of atheist or secular churches, which are popping up around the world. There's the London-based Sunday Assembly London, whose motto is "Live better, help often, wonder more." In 2013, the comedians Sanderson Jones and Pippa Evans realized that they were looking for something that looked like church—full of singing, inspiring talks, and community—but wanted a version of it that was not premised on a belief in God. They decided to hold a secular church service in London to see if others would be interested in something similar. They were: two hundred people showed up for the first meeting and three hundred for the second. Sunday Assembly is now expanding quickly, with forty-five chapters in eight countries so far.

Here in the United States, similar concepts are popping up. There's the Seattle Atheist Church, which explicitly denies the existence of God and features sermons on topics such as the morality of atheism and how atheism is good for one's health. At the North Texas Church of Freethought, nonbelievers receive guidance about how to live among the Bible-thumping friends, family, and neighbors in their community. The Oasis Network has many locations in the Bible Belt, offering a churchlike gathering for people across the spectrum of "nones," including humanists, agnostics, atheists, and even questioning theists. These groups all provide many of the same features as religious congregations, including educational lectures, group discussions, children's programs, and communal meals.

There are also secular events inspired by non-Christian religious traditions. In 2013, a small group of New Yorkers created Pop-Up Shabbat, a communal Friday-night dinner based loosely around the Jewish sabbath meal where people could bond and talk about important issues without any explicit religious teachings. That original group has since dissolved, but it inspired other people to create events with a similar format across the United States and around the world.

There are also online communities that provide a space for people to have profound discussions based on secular texts, for people who don't necessarily believe in God but enjoy the ritual of studying a sacred text. The weekly podcast *Harry Potter and the Sacred Text*, for instance, treats the Harry Potter series as if it were religious scripture. The cohosts, who began the podcast as Harvard Divinity School students, invite listeners to read the books in a group with the same kind of slow, concentrated attention that people typically exert on the Bible. An episode about the Hogwarts Sorting Hat, for instance, becomes a way to discuss how much we control our own fate and how our choices define us.

There are also new options for the many millennials who still believe in God but have been scarred by childhood experiences with churches that are judgmental, political, or dogmatic. These people actually form a large part of the millennial population. Only 13 percent of the religiously unaffiliated accept the identity of "atheist."[15] Half of millennials say they believe in God with absolute certainty, and about 40 percent say religion is very important in their lives.[16] (This is a sizable proportion, but it is a decline from older generations: 59 percent of baby boomers say religion is important to them, and 67 percent of the Silent Generation say the same.) And surprisingly, more than half of "nones" believe in Heaven and Hell.[17]

Even though only a quarter of millennials attend weekly religious services, 42 percent say they pray daily.[18] In fact, many millennials who are not religiously affiliated still feel a strong sense of spirituality. According to a Pew survey, half of all millennials say they feel a sense of spiritual peace and well-being and a sense of wonder about the world at least once a week. Forty-four percent say they spend time thinking about the purpose of life.[19] In other words, young people are finding ways to find spiritual fulfilment without going to church. They're trying to extract the parts of religion they find important and meaningful while leaving behind the parts they find problematic.

Many millennials simply haven't found a church that accurately reflects their beliefs and values but still appreciate religious practices. This has been an ongoing struggle of mine. I am politically and socially progressive, which often puts me at odds with many conservative denominations. I support same-sex marriage and the right to have an abortion and find it troubling when evangelical Christians use the pulpit to campaign against these issues.[20] This is a common feeling among my generation: today's young people are more likely to embrace cultural pluralism and express tolerance for different personal behaviors than their elders are. Since I left home, I've hopped from church to church, searching for one that feels right. I've visited tiny Anglican congregations that incorporate Buddhist chanting and prayer drums, and large charismatic churches where people speak in tongues. I've visited yuppie Presbyterian churches that meet in art galleries and host wine tastings, and Methodist congregations that organize Pride marches and gun control protests.

In the midst of my own church explorations, I've found that millennials are reimagining what church can be in the twenty-first century. In 2018, an Episcopal church in San Francisco hosted a worship service called "Beyoncé Mass" that did not go so far as to deify Queen Bey but used her life and music as a springboard for discussing spiritual issues. The whole event had a joyful, celebratory vibe that brought together more than a thousand people. More Beyoncé Masses are planned around the country in the future. In 2019, a coworking space called the Divine Office opened in Santa Monica as a place for people of any religion to combine daily work with monastic-style contemplation. Members begin and end the workday with prayer and break for a fifteen-minute meditation at noon. The underlying idea is that work and worship are equally sacred.

Others are working to create alternative churches that will attract people week after week. Many of these new churches were started by twentysomethings who felt let down by what mainstream religion had to offer. Take Zach Kerzee, for instance, who grew up in Texas before attending Harvard Divinity School. In 2014, at the age of twenty-five, he decided to create a church in the small town of Grafton, Massachusetts, that better reflects what he believes people are looking for. His concept, Simple Church, doesn't have a building, nor does it meet on Sunday mornings. Instead, he works at an organic farm, where he is paid in vegetables. Every Thursday, he uses this food to make a large dinner, which is hosted at someone's house or in a rented space. The meals are open to anybody, and he makes it clear that LGBTQ people are welcome. About thirty people typically attend. Some are Christian, but others are just there to enjoy the conversation and community.

In Minneapolis, Minnesota, there's a new concept that might best be described as an ecochurch. The New City Church was founded by Tyler Sit in 2015, when he was twenty-six. After attending Emory University's theology school, he came up with a church concept that blends Christianity with environmentalism, an issue that many millennials feel passionate about. He makes the case that faith and our treatment of the planet are deeply connected because Christians believe that the earth is God's creation. Therefore, caring for the earth is a form of worship, and harming it is a sin. The New City Church is equally committed to social justice and believes that climate change and pollution disproportionately affect the poor. The church has organized a network of backyard farms in nearby neighborhoods that generates plenty of fresh produce that is given to people in the community who need it.

HOW FAMILY LIFE MAKES YOU RETHINK FAITH

Ben and I could not have come from more different backgrounds; whereas I come from a family of Christian converts, he comes from a line of atheists. While my family was busy trying to create religious traditions of our own, his family was committed to living a secular life. As a child, I remember carrying a freshly cut Christmas tree home with my mother and putting on a scratchy smocking dress to attend candlelight services on

Christmas Eve. Meanwhile, Ben's family didn't want any religious symbols in their home. In the absence of a Christmas tree or a Hanukkah menorah, they placed holiday presents under the piano.

On our first date, Ben and I sat at a small table at the Hungarian Pastry Shop in New York City. We found it easy to talk to each other, and as we chatted about our families, we found each other's differences intriguing. I was curious about what it was like not only to question God's existence but to believe with certainty that there was no such thing as the divine. Ben, for his part, sometimes came with me to church services to see what happened there. We would talk about the sermons for hours afterward.

It took a few years for our religious differences to become an issue. When our relationship grew more serious, we began to imagine what it would be like to build a family together and realized that we had different ideas about raising children. I knew I wanted to bring up my children with all the religious traditions and practices I had experienced as a child. Ben wasn't sure that he was comfortable with that. I worried what might happen to our imaginary children with our totally divergent faiths: Would they be confused? Would the differences create tension at home? When we entered our midtwenties, all of that was moot, because we had so many other problems at the time that we decided to break up. But those conversations made it clear to us that faith sometimes takes on new meaning in the context of family life.

Barna Group, a think tank that studies faith and culture, found that half of all parents reconsider the question of religion when they have children.[21] About a sixth of them said that having a baby had prompted them to reconnect with church after a long period of not attending. A fifth of parents said that they had already been active but had become even more involved when they had children. Another 4 percent of parents said that having children had actually decreased their involvement in church. But for 5 percent of parents, the experience of having a baby had sparked an entirely new experience of faith.

Confronting death also bears on our religious outlook. Abraham Maslow, the psychologist, said that tragedy and trauma are among the most important learning experiences for humans. They teach us that life is sometimes uncontrollable and uncertain. Like many people, Ben and I experienced our first real brush with death in our twenties, with my father's passing. Ben had been close to my father, even after our breakup, and he was with me the day my father died unexpectedly during heart surgery. He comforted my mother and me in the days that followed, when we were utterly distraught. That moment forced us to reckon with what we believed. For me, it was a time to deepen my faith; Ben, for his part, became more open to a faith he hadn't known before.

He was among the small group of people who discover a new religion in their rocket years that carries with them into adulthood. There's no denying the mass exodus away from Christianity, with 19.2 percent of Americans leaving the church. But a fragment of Americans (4.2 percent) who did not grow up Christian actually choose to convert to Christianity. And another 2.6 percent of the population will convert to non-Christian faiths, such as Judaism, Islam, Buddhism, and Hinduism.[22]

Adopting a new religion puts everything into a new light, from your identity to how you spend your time to the family traditions you establish. For Ben, that transformation happened slowly, over the course of years, as he quietly observed the world in his twenties. By the time we got married, we were largely on the same page when it came to faith. When Ella was born, we baptized her in a Methodist church. A crowd of our friends and relatives of all religious backgrounds showed up. Ben's Jewish aunt came in a large straw hat. One of my friends, a scholar of Hinduism, was able to stop by before jetting off to India. And one of the Baptist missionaries who had first met my parents in their small Malaysian church flew in from South Carolina for the occasion, bringing the story full circle.

THOSE WHO COME BACK

In James Fowler's theory about the stages of faith, he argues that at some point in our lives, very likely in our twenties, we will lose our faith. No matter what beliefs we are raised with, whether they are religious or secular, a time will come when we will reject everything we know to be true about the world. The question is what will happen next. Typically, there are three paths: some of us will never come back, some of us will discover an entirely new religion, and some of us will lose our faith and rediscover some version of it again. It's hard to say exactly how many of us are in this last category. Surveys show that more than half of millennials choose to identify with their childhood religion, but there is also a lot of evidence that many have stopped attending religious services and no longer practice their faith in any sort of meaningful way. Whatever the case, it's clear that religious millennials are a shrinking group.

Research shows that people who remain devout through adulthood tend to be more religious as children and teenagers as well. Pew has found that people who remain lifelong Christians are much more likely to have attended church services regularly and had strong faith between the ages of thirteen and eighteen than are those who went on to abandon their faith.[23] Family dynamics have a part to play as well. Research from the PRRI shows that stable families are more likely to transmit a religious identity to their children, while those raised by divorced parents are more likely to become "nones."[24] Parents who regularly attend religious services are also more likely to pass on their faith to their children. I suspect that many couples are aware of this, which is why religion suddenly becomes a critical discussion when they decide to have children.

My life tracks very closely with these data. I was interested in religion throughout my teens. In high school, dinner table conversations often spiraled into spirited theological debates between my father and me, as we argued about how a good God could allow suffering in the world or questioned each other's interpretation of particular passages of the Bible. It's also clear to me that I was influenced by the faith my parents modeled for me. I grew up observing my father's practice of reading the Bible and writing out his prayers every day. When he passed away, we found a vast store of notebooks that recorded his ongoing conversations with God throughout his life.

But it was also true that all of my religious beliefs would be put to the test over and over once I left home. And in fact, that was what my parents wanted for me. When I was applying to colleges, my parents steered me away from attending a Christian school. My father felt that it was valuable for me to read about, understand, and empathize with many ways of seeing the world, including secular and atheistic perspectives, rather than stay in a religious bubble. Moreover, he thought that if my faith crumbled at the first sign of an intellectual challenge, it couldn't have been very solid to begin with.

As a freshman at Columbia, I reveled in the university's famous Great Books curriculum, where we read the works of thinkers ranging from Plato to Friedrich Nietzsche. I sought out courses on world religions, and was particularly interested in reading the Bhagavad Gita, the Torah, and the Quran. I was sometimes the token Christian in the class, so I found myself constantly trying to demonstrate that it was possible to be a rational, thinking person while still believing in the divine. I offered feminist interpretations of the Bible and pointed to the ways Christians were at the forefront of social justice movements, not just the culture wars. But I don't think I really had to convince my classmates of anything. In the end, I was mostly trying to make the case to myself.

I was constantly wrangling with Christians on campus, many of whom were much more conservative than I was. I read and reread the Bible in an effort to make compelling theological arguments supporting gay rights and challenging gender norms. It was so exhausting that I eventually stopped attending Christian meetings on campus because I clashed so frequently with everyone else there. There were periods when I stopped attending church altogether just to get away from the fray. But I always came back, mostly because I missed the ritual of meditating quietly in the pews.

Like all the other turbulent moments in my twenties, my spiritual crises helped me figure out what it is I really believe and want from life. After leaving many churches, I discovered some congregations that shared my progressive politics. I've now been part of churches that have floats in the Pride parade and provide safe haven to undocumented immigrants. In my thirties, religion is a much more peaceful, restorative part of my life. These days, Ben and I have settled into a nondenominational church with thoughtful teaching that challenges us. It has a well-run nursery, so we can focus on the sermon knowing that Ella is in safe hands. It finally feels like home.

We're now trying to decide how to introduce religion into

our child's life. I'm trying to follow the example my family set for me by modeling my faith for Ella, giving her plenty of opportunities to learn and ask questions but also allowing her space to think through her beliefs for herself.

Then again, she's only three. For now, her main theological concern is the little wooden figures in the Nativity set we bought her on our vacation to Italy. For weeks before Christmas, she delighted in taking out the characters one at a time, first the wise men, then the shepherds, then the angels. She has decided to call the donkey "Bo" for reasons I don't understand, as the sheep and camels in the box remain nameless. But there's something wrong, she tells me, with distress in her voice. In her picture book of the Christmas story, there's a cat playing in the straw next to the manger where baby Jesus sleeps. She digs into the Nativity set but can't find a cat anywhere. "Mommy, where is the cat?" she asks, upset. "We're missing the cat."

I expect that Ella's spiritual questions will get more complicated as she gets older. I hope that when that happens, I will be able to provide thoughtful, satisfying answers. But for now, I really need to find a little wooden cat.

EPILOGUE

It's just another Wednesday night. We've just had grilled chicken and couscous for dinner. While Ben washes the dishes, I put Ella to sleep.

Bedtime is easier now than it was two years ago, partly because Ella is now old enough to brush her own teeth and partly because I'm getting the hang of this parenting thing. Tonight I read her a story about dinosaurs; then we flip through a picture book about Ruth Bader Ginsburg. Ella makes me arrange, then rearrange, the stuffed animals at the edge of her bed: Bunny next to Doggy next to Tilly, the elephant. She asks me to make sure her pink flashlight is within her reach in case she gets scared of the dark. I kiss her good night, switch off the lights, and meander downstairs to sit on the sofa with Ben.

In some ways, our lives have not changed much since we entered our thirties. There's less chaos, more routine. At the same time, things are forever in flux. For one thing, we're sitting on a different sofa in a different house. Over the past two years, we've moved from Boston to Florida, then back to Boston again. We've lived in three homes, explored new neighborhoods, voted in different precincts. I've astonished myself by becoming a bit of a gym rat. My friend Tara is flying in from Tallahassee to spend the weekend with me.

Life is always moving forward. Things slow down a bit after your twenties, the momentum of those tumultuous years carrying you toward the ones to come. But there are plenty more chapters of your story to write. There are relationships to create, nurture, and deepen. There are new goals to reach for in your career. There are new dimensions of your identity to explore, new interests to discover, new people to meet. I still dream of scaling Annapurna. Perhaps I'll take a wilderness training course this summer.

We have more power over our lives than our ancestors ever dared dream of. My own grandmother never went to school. Her marriage to my grandfather was arranged. She was expected to become a mother, so she had six children. In her old age, I remember her beaming with love and contentment. She had a good life, but it was largely scripted for her.

That is not my reality. In our time, we get to write our own stories. We can fall in love and marry our soul mates. We can ponder our passions, then find work and pastimes that fulfill them. We can imagine and create the kind of family we want to carry us through life. Ultimately, the work of your twenties, with all its glorious potential, is to take the first massive steps toward establishing who you are. The abundance of choice is thrilling, but it can also be overwhelming. It's easy to worry that we will squander opportunities and close doors and make mistakes we will never recover from. But our rocket years aren't about getting everything right or wrong. Succeeding or failing. Moving ahead or falling behind. They're about creating a sense of self. So give yourself the space and time to think through what you want your life to be.

And if I can leave you with one last thought, it is this: You keep editing your story long after your twenties. The decisions you make in your rocket years are an important starting point, but you have the rest of your life to bring in new characters, introduce surprising plot twists, and continually reinvent yourself.

Now put this book down and get out into the world. You have a masterpiece to create.

ACKNOWLEDGMENTS

Ben, you are my world. Thank you for making my life, and this book, possible. When I was looking for a new career challenge, you sat with me in that ramen shop to brainstorm ideas. You helped me find data, you read draft after draft, you watched Ella for the better part of a year to give me time to write. You have always believed I can do anything and, more than that, you do everything it takes to allow me to turn my dreams into reality. I am so happy I knocked on your door that night when we were eighteen. Just look at this marvelous life we've created together!

Ella, you are the great love of my life. You fill my world with laughter and joy, and spur me to be the best version of myself. So many stories in this book were inspired by you. I cannot wait for all the adventures we'll have in the years to come.

Mom, thank you for sharing your gift of writing with me and modeling what it means to build a life as a writer. I am so happy that you're continuing to throw yourself into your craft and turn your incredible life experiences into volumes of stories. Papa would be so happy to see the life you've created here in the United States and he would be proud of your award-winning body of work.

ACKNOWLEDGMENTS

This book would not have been possible without my agent and friend, Andrew Stuart, who reached out to me before this book was even a twinkle in my eye. Thank you for believing in me and my ideas, and for fighting hard on my behalf every step of the way. It means so much to me that you respond to every one of my panicked emails and calls immediately, and offer a constant stream of kindness and support. I look forward to many more long chats at coffee shops around New York.

Many thanks to everyone at HarperCollins who made this book possible, especially Hannah Robinson, Haley Swanson, Sarah Lambert, Emily VanDerwerken, Lydia Weaver, and Elina Cohen.

I could not have written this book without the love and support of my community. Thank you Joyce Ng, Steve Dry, Katie Carlone, Kathy Hess, Tara Gardner, and Fiona Hayman for reading through drafts, then offering detailed feedback and comments. Thank you Adrianne Wright, Leland Drummond, Sali Christeson, and Colleen Flynn—my league of powerful women—for believing in this book, and helping me get the word out about it. And finally, to my editors at *Fast Company*, particularly Kate Davis, Suzanne LaBarre, and Kelsey Campbell-Dolloghan, thank you for being so encouraging of this project, and filling my daily life at the office with so much positivity.

Introduction

1. The poet Mary Oliver famously asked the question in her poem "The Summer Day."

Chapter One: Career

1. "Millennial Careers: 2020 Vision," ManpowerGroup, 2016, https://manpowergroup.us/campaigns/manpower/millennial-careers/pdf/MPG_NAMillennials2020VisionWhitPr5_20_16.pdf.

2. Brandon Rigoni and Amy Adkins, "What Millennials Want from a New Job," *Harvard Business Review*, May 11, 2016, https://hbr.org/2016/05/what-millennials-want-from-a-new-job.

3. Nina McQueen, "Workplace Culture Trends: The Key to Hiring (and Keeping) Top Talent in 2018," LinkedIn Official Blog, June 26, 2018, https://blog.linkedin.com/2018/june/26/workplace-culture-trends-the-key-to-hiring-and-keeping-top-talent.

4. Rigoni and Adkins, "What Millennials Want from a New Job."

5. "Millennials in the Workplace: Does Father Still Know Best?," LinkedIn, September 18, 2013, https://www.slideshare.net/PGi/millennials-in-t.

6. Ibid.

7. Derek Thompson, "Workism Is Making Americans Miserable," *The Atlantic*, February 24, 2019, https://www.theatlantic.com/ideas/archive/2019/02/religion-workism-making-americans-miserable/583441.

8. Juliana Menasce Horowitz and Nikki Graf, "Most U.S. Teens See Anxiety, Depression as a Major Problem among Their Peers," Pew Research Center, February 20, 2019, https://www.pewsocialtrends.org/2019/02/20/most-u-s-teens-see-anxiety-and-depression-as-a-major-problem-among-their-peers/.

9. Amy Adkins, "Millennials: The Job-Hopping Generation," Gallup, May 12, 2016, https://www.gallup.com/workplace/231587/millennials-job-hopping-generation.aspx.

10. Sarah Berger, "Most Workers Leave Paid Vacation Time Unused, a Bankrate Survey Finds," Bankrate, December 19, 2016, https://www.bankrate.com/finance/consumer-index/money-pulse-1216.aspx.

11. "Under-Vacationed America: A State-by-State Look at Time Off," U.S. Travel Association, August 8, 2018, https://www.ustravel.org/research/under-vacationed-america-state-state-look-time.

12. Anne Helen Petersen, "How Millennials Became the Burnout Generation," BuzzFeed News, January 5, 2019, https://www.buzzfeednews.com/article/annehelenpetersen/millennials-burnout-generation-debt-work.

13. Steve Jobs, "'You've Got to Find What You Love,' Jobs Says," *Stanford News*, June 14, 2005, https://news.stanford.edu/2005/06/14/jobs-061505/.

14. "2018 Workforce Mindset Study," Alight, December 4, 2018, https://ideas.alight.com/workforce-mindset/2018-workforce-mindset-study.

15. "How Millennials Want to Work and Live," Gallup, May 2016, https://www.gallup.com/workplace/238073/millennials-work-live.aspx.

16. Norman B. Anderson, Cynthia D. Belar, Steven J. Breckler, et al., "Stress in America: Paying with Our Health," American Psychological Association, February 4, 2015, https://www.apa.org/news/press/releases/stress/2014/stress-report.pdf.

17. Amy Westervelt, "Happy Employees Are Healthier (and Cheaper)," *The Guardian*, June 18, 2014, https://www.theguardian.com /sustainable-business/2014/jun/18/happy-employees-are-healthier -and-cheaper.

18. Benjamin Todd, "We Reviewed Over 60 Studies about What Makes for a Dream Job. Here's What We Found," 80,000 Hours, April 2017, https://80000hours.org/career-guide/job-satisfaction/.

19. "Number of Jobs Held, Labor Market Activity, and Earnings Growth Among the Youngest Baby Boomers: Results from a Longitudinal Survey Summary," Bureau of Labor Statistics, August 24, 2017, http://web.archive.org/web/20170829000339/https://www.bls.gov /news.release/nlsoy.nr0.htm.

20. "How Millennials Want to Work and Live."

21. Nathan Hellman, "4 Essential Questions Everyone Should Ask about Job Hopping," *U.S. News & World Report*, May 2, 2016, https://money.usnews.com/careers/articles/2016-05-02/4 -essential-questions-everyone-should-ask-about-job-hopping.

22. Ibid.

23. Ibid.

24. Kelly Steenackers and Marie-Anne Guerry, "Determinants of Job-Hopping: An Empirical Study in Belgium," *International Journal of Manpower* 37, no. 3 (2016): 494–510.

25. Bruce Fallick, Charles A. Fleischman, and James B. Rebitzer, "Job-Hopping in Silicon Valley: Some Evidence Concerning the Microfoundations of a High-Technology Cluster," *Review of Economics and Statistics* 88, no. 3 (February 2006): 472–81.

26. Shujaat Farooq, "Mismatch Between Education and Occupation: A Case Study of Pakistani Graduates," *The Pakistan Development Review*, December 2011, 531–52.

27. Douglas C. Maynard, Todd Allen Joseph, and Amanda M. Maynard, "Underemployment, Job Attitudes, and Turnover Intentions," *Journal of Organizational Behavior* 27, no. 4 (June 2006): 509–36.

28. Frances M. McKee-Ryan and Jaron Harvey, "'I Have a Job, but . . .': A Review of Underemployment," *Journal of Management* 37, no. 4 (2011): 962–96.

29. Stephen Rubb, "Overeducation: A Short or Long Run Phenomenon for Individuals?," *Economics of Education Review* 22, no. 4 (August 2003): 389–94.

30. McKee-Ryan and Harvey, "'I Have a Job, but . . .'"

31. David Dooley, Joann Prause, and Kathleen A. Ham-Rowbottom, "Underemployment and Depression: Longitudinal Relationships," *Journal of Health and Social Behavior* 41, no. 4 (December 2000): 421–36.

32. McKee-Ryan and Harvey, "'I Have a Job, but . . .'"

33. "Freelancing in America 2018," Upwork, October 31, 2018, https://www.upwork.com/i/freelancing-in-america.

34. Ibid.

35. Ibid.

36. Ibid.

37. Ibid.

38. Kelly Monahan, Tiffany Schleeter, and Jeff Schwartz, "Decoding Millennials in the Gig Economy: Six Trends to Watch in Alternative Work," Deloitte, May 1, 2018, https://www2.deloitte.com/insights/us/en/focus/technology-and-the-future-of-work/millennials-in-the-gig-economy.html.

39. Ibid.

40. "Freelancing in America 2018."

41. Ibid.

42. Hironao Okahana and Enyu Zhou, "Graduate Enrollment and Degrees: 2007 to 2017," Council of Graduate Schools, October 2018, https://cgsnet.org/ckfinder/userfiles/files/CGS_GED17_Report.pdf.

43. Jordan Weissmann, "How Many Ph.D.s Actually Get to Become College Professors?," *The Atlantic*, February 23, 2013, https://www.theatlantic.com/business/archive/2013/02/how-many-phds-actually-get-to-become-college-professors/273434/.

44. Laura McKenna, "The Ever-Tightening Job Market for Ph.D.s," *The Atlantic*, April 21, 2016, https://www.theatlantic.com/education/archive/2016/04/bad-job-market-phds/479205/.

45. Sandy Baum and Patricia Steele, "Who Goes to Graduate School and Who Succeeds?," Urban Institute, April 6, 2017, https://www.ssrn.com/abstract2898458.

46. America Counts Staff, "Number of People with Master's and Doctoral Degrees Doubles Since 2000," United States Census Bureau, February 21, 2019, https://www.census.gov/library/stories/2019/02/number-of-people-with-masters-and-phd-degrees-double-since-2000.html.

47. Baum and Steele, "Who Goes to Graduate School and Who Succeeds?"

48. Laura Pappano, "The Master's as the New Bachelor's," *New York Times*, July 22, 2011, https://www.nytimes.com/2011/07/24/education/edlife/edl-24masters-t.html.

49. "How America Pays for Graduate School," Sallie Mae, 2017, https://www.salliemae.com/assets/Research/HAPGS/HAPGRAD_SchoolReport.pdf.

50. "Cumulative Debt: Undergraduate Degree Recipients," College Board, 2018 https://research.collegeboard.org/pdf/01469-061-trends-saf15f16f17.pdf.

51. "Data on Certifications and Licenses," Bureau of Labor Statistics, January 18, 2019, https://www.bls.gov/cps/certifications-and-licenses.htm.

52. Jennifer González, "Certificates Rise to 22% of Postsecondary Credentials Awarded, Report Says," *The Chronicle of Higher Education*, June 6, 2012, https://www.chronicle.com/article/Certificates-Rise-to-22-of/132143.

53. Baum and Steele, "Who Goes to Graduate School and Who Succeeds?"

54. Zac Auter, "Few MBA, Law Grads Say Their Degree Prepared Them Well," Gallup, February 16, 2018, https://news.gallup.com/poll/227039/few-mba-law-grads-say-degree-prepared.aspx.

55. Baum and Steele, "Who Goes to Graduate School and Who Succeeds?"

56. "Class of 2011 National Summary Report," National Association for Law Placement, 2012, https://www.nalp.org/uploads/NatlSummChart_Classof2011.pdf.

57. Ilana Kowarski, "Find MBAs That Lead to Employment, High Salaries,"

U.S. News & World Report, March 13, 2019, https://www.usnews .com/education/best-graduate-schools/top-business-schools/articles /mba-salary-jobs.

Chapter Two: Hobbies

1. Steven M. Gelber, *Hobbies: Leisure and the Culture of Work in America* (New York: Columbia University Press, 1999).

2. Seppo E. Iso-Ahola, "Basic Dimensions of Definitions of Leisure," *Journal of Leisure Research* 11, no. 1 (1979): 28–39; Michael J. Manfredo, B. L. Driver, and Michael A. Tarrant, "Measuring Leisure Motivation: A Meta-Analysis of the Recreation Experience Preference Scales," *Journal of Leisure Research* 28, no. 3 (1996): 188–213, https://www.nrpa.org/globalassets/journals/jlr/1996/volume-28 /jlr-volume-28-number-3-pp-188-213.pdf; Sherry L. Dupuis and Bryan J. A. Smale, "An Examination of Relationship between Psychological Well-Being and Depression and Leisure Activity Participation Among Older Adults," *Loisir et Société/Society and Leisure* 18, no. 1 (1995): 67–92; M. Powell Lawton, "Personality and Affective Correlates of Leisure Activity Participation by Older People," *Journal of Leisure Research* 26, no. 2 (1994): 138–57; K. L. Siegenthaler and Jacquelyn Vaughan, "Older Women in Retirement Communities: Perceptions of Recreation and Leisure," *Leisure Sciences* 20, no. 1 (1998): 53–66.

3. Matthew J. Zawadzki, Joshua M. Smyth, and Heather J. Costigan, "Real-Time Associations between Engaging in Leisure and Daily Health and Well-Being," *Annals of Behavioral Medicine* 49, no. 4 (August 2015): 605–15.

4. Anne Pilon, "Hobbies Survey: Most Have Made Hobby Related Purchases," AYTM, January 12, 2016, https://aytm.com/blog/hobbies -survey/.

5. "American Time Use Survey—2016 Microdata Files," Bureau of Labor Statistics, July 20, 2017, https://www.bls.gov/tus/datafiles _2016.htm.

6. Neda Agahi, Kozma Ahacic, and Marti G. Parker, "Continuity of Leisure Participation From Middle Age to Old Age," *The Journals of Gerontology, Series B* 61, no. 6 (November 2006): S340–46.

7. See, e.g., Robert C. Atchley, "A Continuity Theory of Normal Aging," *The Gerontologist* 29, no. 2 (April 1989): 183–90, https://academic.oup.com/gerontologist/article-abstract/29/2/183/581908?redirectedFrom=fulltext.

8. Larissa Faw, "Mobile Internet Usage Reaches 800 Hours a Year," MediaPost Agency Daily, June 10, 2019, https://www.mediapost.com/publications/article/336807/mobile-internet-usage-reaches-800-hours-a-year.html.

9. Ibid.

10. Mark Aguiar and Erik Hurst, "Measuring Trends in Leisure: The Allocation of Time over Five Decades," *The Quarterly Journal of Economics* 122, no. 3 (August 2007): 969–1006.

11. Andrew Van Dam and Eric Morath, "Changing Times," *The Wall Street Journal*, June 24, 2016, https://graphics.wsj.com/time-use/.

12. Michael Bittman and Judy Wajcman, "The Rush Hour: The Character of Leisure Time and Gender Equity," *Social Forces* 79, no. 1 (September 2000): 165–89.

13. Jose Ignacio Gimenez-Nadal and Almudena Sevilla-Sanz, "The Time-Crunch Paradox," *Social Indicators Research* 102, no. 2 (June 2011): 181–96.

14. Almudena Sevilla, Jose I. Gimenez-Nadal, and Jonathan Gershuny, "Leisure Inequality in the United States: 1965–2003," *Demography* 49, no. 3 (2012): 939–64.

15. Derek Thompson, "Workism Is Making Americans Miserable," *The Atlantic*, February 24, 2019, https://www.theatlantic.com/ideas/archive/2019/02/religion-workism-making-americans-miserable/583441.

16. Denise C. Park, Jennifer Lodi-Smith, Linda Drew, et al., "The Impact of Sustained Engagement on Cognitive Function in Older Adults: The Synapse Project," *Psychological Science* 25, no. 1 (2014): 103–12, https://www.ncbi.nlm.nih.gov/pmc/articles/PMC4154531/.

17. Valorie N. Salimpoor, Mitchel Benovoy, Kevin Larcher, et al., "Anatomically Distinct Dopamine Release During Anticipation and Experience of Peak Emotion to Music," *Nature Neuroscience* 14, no. 2 (February 2011): 257–62.

Chapter Three: Fitness

1. Carl J. Caspersen, Mark A. Pereira, and Katy M. Curran, "Changes in Physical Activity Patterns in the United States, by Sex and Cross-sectional Age," *Medicine & Science in Sports & Exercise* 32, no. 9 (September 2000): 1601–09.

2. "The Health of Millennials," BlueCross BlueShield, April 24, 2019, https://www.bcbs.com/the-health-of-america/reports/the-health-of -millennials.

3. Katie Heaney, "So What Really Happens to Your Metabolism After 30?," *New York*, August 20, 2018, https://www.thecut.com/2018/08 /how-much-does-metabolism-drop-after-age-30.html.

4. Shichun Du, Tamim Raijo, Sylvia Santosa, and Michael D. Jensen, "The Thermic Effect of Food Is Reduced in Older Adults," *Hormone and Metabolic Research* 46, no. 5 (May 2014): 365–69.

5. Sharon A. Simpson, Christine Shaw, and Rachel McNamara, "What Is the Most Effective Way to Maintain Weight Loss in Adults?," *The British Medical Journal* 343 (2011): d8042.

6. Victoria A. Catenacci, Lorraine G. Ogden, Jennifer Stuht, et al., "Physical Activity Patterns in the National Weight Control Registry," *Obesity* 16, no. 1 (January 2008): 153–61, https://onlinelibrary.wiley .com/doi/pdf/10.1038/oby.2007.6.

7. Rena R. Wing, "Physical Activity in the Treatment of the Adult-hood Overweight and Obesity: Current Evidence and Research Issues," *Medicine & Science in Sports & Exercise* 31, no. 11 (November 1999): S547–52.

8. Amudha S. Poobalan, Lorna S. Aucott, Amanda Clarke, and William Cairns S. Smith, "Diet Behaviour among Young People in Transition to Adulthood (18–25 Year Olds): A Mixed Method Study," *Health Psychology & Behavioral Medicine* 2, no. 1 (2014): 909–28, http:// citeseerx.ist.psu.edu/viewdoc/download?doi=10.1.1.790.9085 &rep=rep1&type=pdf.

9. Lukas Schwingshackl, Sofia Dias, and Georg Hoffmann, "Impact of Long-Term Lifestyle Programmes on Weight Loss and Cardiovascular Risk Factors in Overweight/Obese Participants: A Systematic

Review and Network Meta-analysis," *Systematic Reviews* 3, no. 1 (2014): 130.

10. Ralph S. Paffenbarger, Robert Hyde, Alvin L. Wing, and Chung-cheng Hsieh, "Physical Activity, All-Cause Mortality, and Longevity of College Alumni," *The New England Journal of Medicine* 314, no. 10 (March 6, 1986): 605–13.

11. Caspersen, Pereira, and Curran, "Changes in Physical Activity Patterns in the United States."

12. Ibid.

13. Shawn C. Sorenson, Russell Romano, Stanley P. Azen, et al., "Life Span Exercise among Elite Intercollegiate Student Athletes," *Sports Health* 7, no. 1 (January 2015): 80–86, https://doi.org/10.1177/1941738114534813.

14. Ibid.

15. "The Health of Millennials."

16. Vivian Giang, "What It Takes to Change Your Brain's Patterns after Age 25," *Fast Company*, April 28, 2015, https://www.fastcompany.com/3045424/what-it-takes-to-change-your-brains-patterns-after-age-25.

17. Bruno Dubuc, The Brain from Top to Bottom, "Plasticity in Neural Networks," May 2012, https://thebrain.mcgill.ca/flash/d/d_07/d_7_cl/d_07_cl_tra/d_07_cl_tra.html.

18. Giang, "What It Takes To Change Your Brain's Patterns after Age 25."

19. Ibid.

20. Charles Duhigg, "How to Form Healthy Habits in Your 20s," *New York Times*, October 18, 2016, https://www.nytimes.com/2016/10/19/well/mind/how-to-form-healthy-habits-in-your-20s.html.

21. Ibid.

22. John Donvan, "The 'Power' to Trade Naughty Habits for Nice Ones," *Talk of the Nation*, National Public Radio, December 24, 2012, https://www.npr.org/2012/12/24/167977418/the-power-to-trade-naughty-habits-for-nice-ones.

Chapter Four: Marriage

1. A. W. Geiger and Gretchen Livingston, "8 Facts About Love and Marriage in America," Pew Research Center, February 13, 2019, https://www.pewresearch.org/fact-tank/2019/02/13/8-facts-about-love-and-marriage/.

2. Ibid.

3. Meg Murphy, "NowUKnow: Why Millennials Refuse to Get Married," Bentley University, https://www.bentley.edu/news/nowuknow-why-millennials-refuse-get-married.

4. "Historical Marital Status Tables," United States Census Bureau, November 2018, https://www.census.gov/data/tables/time-series/demo/families/marital.html.

5. Roni Caryn Rabin, "Put a Ring on It? Millennial Couples Are in No Hurry," New York Times, May 29, 2018, https://www.nytimes.com/2018/05/29/well/mind/millennials-love-marriage-sex-relationships-dating.html.

6. Stephanie Coontz, Marriage, a History: How Love Conquered Marriage (New York: Penguin, 2006), 15.

7. Ibid., 19.

8. William M. Kephart, "Some Correlates of Romantic Love," Journal of Marriage and Family 29, no. 3 (August 1967): 470–74, https://doi.org/10.2307/349585.

9. "Table A-1. Employment Status of the Civilian Population by Sex and Age," Bureau of Labor Statistics, https://www.bls.gov/news.release/empsit.t01.htm.

10. Mark DeWolf, "12 Stats About Working Women," U.S. Department of Labor Blog, March 1, 2017, https://blog.dol.gov/2017/03/01/12-stats-about-working-women.

11. "Most Want a Partner like Them," Monmouth University Polling Institute, February 9, 2017, https://www.monmouth.edu/polling-institute/reports/monmouthpoll_us_020917/.

12. Philip N. Cohen, "The Coming Divorce Decline," Socius, August 28, 2019, https://journals.sagepub.com/doi/full/10.1177/2378023119873497.

13. Geiger and Livingston, "8 Facts About Love and Marriage in America."

14. Wendy Wang and Kim Parker, "Record Share of Americans Have Never Married," Pew Research Center, September 24, 2014, https://www.pewsocialtrends.org/2014/09/24/record-share-of-americans-have-never-married/.

15. Benjamin Gurrentz, "For Young Adults, Cohabitation Is Up, Marriage Is Down," United States Census Bureau, November 15, 2018, https://www.census.gov/library/stories/2018/11/cohabitaiton-is-up-marriage-is-down-for-young-adults.html.

16. *A Survey of LGBT Americans: Attitudes, Experiences and Values in Changing Times*, Pew Research Center, June 13, 2013, https://www.pewsocialtrends.org/wp-content/uploads/sites/3/2013/06/SDT_LGBT-Americans_06-2013.pdf, chap. 4.

17. Ibid.

18. Seth Williams, "Child Poverty in the United States, 2010," NCFMR Family Profiles, National Center for Family & Marriage Research, 2012, http://www.bgsu.edu/content/dam/BGSU/college-of-arts-and-sciences/NCFMR/documents/FP/FP-12-17.pdf.

19. William Bradford Wilcox, "Why Marriage Matters, Third Edition: Thirty Conclusions from the Social Sciences," Institute for American Values, 2011, https://irp-cdn.multiscreensite.com/64484987/files/uploaded/Why-Marriage-Matters-Third-Edition-FINAL.pdf.

20. *A Survey of LGBT Americans*, chap. 4.

21. Allison Linn, "Why Married People Tend to Be Wealthier: It's Complicated," *Today*, February 13, 2013, http://www.today.com/money/why-married-people-tend-be-wealthier-its-complicated-1C8364877.

22. Linda J. Waite and Maggie Gallagher, *The Case for Marriage: Why Married People Are Happier, Healthier, and Better Off Financially* (New York: Penguin Random House, 2001).

23. Robert H. Shmerling, "The Health Advantages of Marriage," Harvard Health Blog, November 30, 2016, https://www.health.harvard.edu/blog/the-health-advantages-of-marriage-2016113010667.

24. Ibid.

25. Wang and Parker, "Record Share of Americans Have Never Married."

26. "Most Want a Partner like Them."

27. Ibid.

28. Shanhong Luo and Eva C. Klohnen, "Assortative Mating and Marital Quality in Newlyweds: A Couple-Centered Approach," *Journal of Personality and Social Psychology* 88, no. 2 (2005): 304–26, https://www.apa.org/pubs/journals/releases/psp-882304.pdf.

29. A. Tognetti, C. Berticat, M. Raymond, and C. Faurie, "Assortative Mating Based on Cooperativeness and Generosity," *Journal of Evolutionary Biology* 27, no. 5 (2014): 975–81, https://doi.org/10.1111/jeb .12346.

30. Sofus Attila Macskassy and Lada Adamic, "From Classmates to Soulmates," Facebook, October 7, 2013, https://www.facebook.com /notes/facebook-data-science/from-classmates-to-soulmates /10151779448773859.

31. Reuben J. Thomas, "Online Exogamy Reconsidered: Estimating the Internet's Effects on Racial, Educational, Religious, Political and Age Assortative Mating," *Social Forces*, May 24, 2019, https://academic.oup.com/sf/advance-article/doi/10.1093/sf/soz060/5498124.

32. Luo and Klohnen, "Assortative Mating and Marital Quality in Newlyweds."

33. "Most Want a Partner like Them."

34. Mikhila N. Humbad, M. Brent Donnellan, William G. Iacono, et al., "Is Spousal Similarity for Personality a Matter of Convergence or Selection?," *Personality and Individual Differences* 49, no. 7 (November 2010): 827–30, https://www.ncbi.nlm.nih.gov/pmc /articles/PMC2992433/.

35. Michael Rosenfeld, Reuben J. Thomas, and Sonia Hausen, "Disintermediating Your Friends: How Dating in the United States Displaces Other Ways of Meeting," *Proceedings of the National Academy of Sciences of the United States of America* 116, no. 36 (September 3, 2019): 17753–58.

36. Helen Fisher and Justin R. Garcia, "Singles in America," Match
.com, https://www.singlesinamerica.com/.

37. Michael J. Rosenfeld, Reuben J. Thomas, and Maja Falcon, "How
Couples Meet and Stay Together (HCMST), Wave 1 2009, Wave 2
2010, Wave 3 2011, Wave 4 2013, Wave 5 2015, United States: Version 8," ICPSR, 2011, https://www.icpsr.umich.edu/icpsrweb/ICPSR
/studies/30103/version/8.

38. Christine R. Schwartz and Robert D. Mare, "Trends in Educational
Assortative Marriage from 1940 to 2003," *Demography* 42, no. 4
(November 2005): 621–46.

39. Ken-Hou Lin and Jennifer Lundquist, "Mate Selection in Cyber-
space: The Intersection of Race, Gender, and Education," *American
Journal of Sociology* 119, no. 1 (July 2013): 183–215.

40. Shauna B. Wilson, William D. McIntosh, and Salvatore P. Insana II,
"Dating Across Race: An Examination of African American Inter-
net Personal Advertisements," *Journal of Black Studies* 37, no. 6
(July 2007): 964–82.

41. Andrew T. Fiore and Judith S. Donath, "Homophily in Online Dat-
ing: When Do You Like Someone Like Yourself?," in *CHI EA '05
Extended Abstracts on Human Factors in Computing Systems* (New
York: ACM, 2005), 1371–74.

42. Ashton Anderson, Sharad Goel, Gregory Huber, et al., "Political Ideology and Racial Preferences in Online Dating," *Sociological Science* 1 (February 18, 2014): 28–40, https://www.sociologicalscience
.com/download/volume%201/february_/Political%20Ideological
%20and%20Racial%20Preferences%20in%20Online%20Dating
.pdf.

43. Michael J. Rosenfeld, "Racial, Educational and Religious Endogamy
in the United States: A Comparative Historical Perspective," *Social
Forces* 87, no. 1 (2008): 1–32, https://web.stanford.edu/~mrosenfe
/Rosenfeld_Endogamy_Comparative_Perspective.pdf.

44. Elizabeth E. Bruch and M. E. J. Newman, "Aspirational Pursuit of
Mates in Online Dating Markets," *Science Advances* 4, no. 8 (August
2018): eaap9815.

45. Aziz Ansari, *Modern Romance:* (New York: Penguin, 2015), 147.

46. Gurrentz, "For Young Adults, Cohabitation Is Up, Marriage Is Down."

47. Quoctrung Bui and Claire Cain Miller, "The Age That Women Have Babies: How a Gap Divides America," *New York Times*, August 4, 2018, https://www.nytimes.com/interactive/2018/08/04/upshot/up-birth-age-gap.html.

48. Nicholas H. Wolfinger, "Replicating the Goldilocks Theory of Marriage and Divorce," Institute for Family Studies, July 20, 2015, https://ifstudies.org/blog/replicating-the-goldilocks-theory-of-marriage-and-divorce.

49. Nicholas H. Wolfinger, "Want to Avoid Divorce? Wait to Get Married, but Not Too Long," Institute for Family Studies, July 16, 2015, https://ifstudies.org/blog/want-to-avoid-divorce-wait-to-get-married-but-not-too-long.

50. Caroline Lester, "Marriage: 'A Luxury Good'?," WGBH News, June 6, 2016, https://www.wgbh.org/news/2016/06/06/innovation-hub-podcast/marriage-luxury-good.

51. David T. Ellwood and Christopher Jencks, "The Spread of Single-Parent Families in the United States Since 1960," in *The Future of the Family*, ed. Daniel Patrick Moynihan, Timothy Smeeding, and Lee Rainwater (New York: Russell Sage Foundation, 2004), 25–65.

52. Francine D. Blau and Anne E. Winkler, "Women, Work, and Family," in *The Oxford Handbook of Women and the Economy*, ed. Susan L. Averett, Laura M. Argys, and Saul D. Hoffman (Oxford University Press, 2018), 395–424.

53. Fisher and Garcia, "Singles in America."

54. Victor Tan Chen, "All Hollowed Out: The Lonely Poverty of America's White Working Class," *The Atlantic*, January 16, 2016, https://www.theatlantic.com/business/archive/2016/01/white-working-class-poverty/424341/.

55. Kim Parker and Renee Stepler, "Americans See Men as the Financial Providers, Even as Women's Contributions Grow," Pew Research Center, September 20, 2017, https://www.pewresearch.org/fact-tank/2017/09/20/americans-see-men-as-the-financial-providers-even-as-womens-contributions-grow/.

56. David Autor, David Dorn, and Gordon Hanson, "When Work Disappears: Manufacturing Decline and the Falling Marriage Market Value of Young Men," *American Economic Review: Insights* 1, no. 7 (September 2019): 161–78.

57. Lester, "Marriage."

58. Casey E. Copen, Kimberly Daniels, Jonathan Vespa, and William D. Mosher, "First Marriages in the United States: Data from the 2006–2010 National Survey of Family Growth," U.S. Department of Health and Human Services, March 22, 2012, https://www.cdc.gov/nchs/data/nhsr/nhsr049.pdf.

59. Wendy Wang, "Early Marriage Has Fallen, Especially among Those without a College Degree," Institute for Family Studies, March 16, 2018, https://ifstudies.org/blog/early-marriage-has-fallen-especially-among-those-without-a-college-degree.

60. Claire Cain Miller and Quoctrung Bui, "Equality in Marriages Grows, and So Does Class Divide," *New York Times*, February 27, 2016, https://www.nytimes.com/2016/02/23/upshot/rise-in-marriages-of-equals-and-in-division-by-class.html.

61. Claire Cain Miller, "Single Motherhood, in Decline over All, Rises for Women 35 and Older," *New York Times*, May 8, 2015, https://www.nytimes.com/2015/05/09/upshot/out-of-wedlock-births-are-falling-except-among-older-women.html.

62. Lester, "Marriage."

Chapter Five: Family

1. Claire Cain Miller, "The U.S. Fertility Rate Is Down, Yet More Women Are Mothers," *New York Times*, January 18, 2018, https://www.nytimes.com/2018/01/18/upshot/the-us-fertility-rate-is-down-yet-more-women-are-mothers.html.

2. Sarah R. Hayford, "The Evolution of Fertility Expectations over the Life Course," *Demography* 46, no. 4 (November 2009): 765–83, https://link.springer.com/article/10.1353%2Fdem.0.0073.

3. Kristen Bialik, "Middle Children Have Become Rarer, but a Growing Share of Americans Now Say Three or More Kids Are 'Ideal,'"

Pew Research Center, August 9, 3018, https://www.pewresearch
.org/fact-tank/2018/08/09/middle-children-have-become-rarer-but
-a-growing-share-of-americans-now-say-three-or-more-kids-are
-ideal/.

4. Claire Cain Miller, "Americans Are Having Fewer Babies. They
Told Us Why," *New York Times*, July 5, 2018, https://www.nytimes
.com/2018/07/05/upshot/americans-are-having-fewer-babies
-they-told-us-why.html.

5. Nan Marie Astone, Steven Martin, and H. Elizabeth Peters,
"Millennial Childbearing and the Recession," Urban Institute,
April 2015, https://www.urban.org/sites/default/files/publication
/49796/2000203-Millennial-Childbearing-and-the-Recession.pdf.

6. "The Cost of Having a Baby in the United States; Executive Summary," Truven Health Analytics, January 2013, http://transform
.childbirthconnection.org/wp-content/uploads/2013/01/Cost
-of-Having-a-Baby-Executive-Summary.pdf.

7. Mark Lino, "The Cost of Raising a Child," U.S. Department of
Agriculture, January 13, 2017, https://www.usda.gov/media/blog
/2017/01/13/cost-raising-child.

8. Miller, "Americans Are Having Fewer Babies."

9. Thomas Hansen, "Parenthood and Happiness: A Review of Folk
Theories versus Empirical Evidence," *Social Indicators Research*
108, no. 1 (August 2012): 29–64, https://link.springer.com/article/1
0.1007%2Fs11205-011-9865-y.

10. Jean M. Twenge, W. Keith Campbell, and Craig A. Foster, "Parenthood and Marital Satisfaction: A Meta-analytic Review," *Journal of
Marriage and Family* 65, no. 3 (August 2003): 574–83.

11. Jennifer Senior, *All Joy and No Fun: The Paradox of Modern Parenthood* (New York: Ecco, 2014).

12. Gretchen Livingston, "For Most Highly Educated Women, Motherhood Doesn't Start Until the 30s," Pew Research Center, January
2015, https://www.pewresearch.org/fact-tank/2015/01/15/for-most
-highly-educated-women-motherhood-doesnt-start-until-the-30s/.

13. Lino, "The Cost of Raising a Child."

14. "Miscarriage," March of Dimes, 2019, https://www.marchofdimes .org/complications/miscarriage.aspx.

15. Kim Parker, "Women More than Men Adjust Their Careers for Family Life," Pew Research Center, October 1, 2015, https://www .pewresearch.org/fact-tank/2015/10/01/women-more-than-men -adjust-their-careers-for-family-life/.

16. "Married Parents' Use of Time Summary," Bureau of Labor Statistics, May 8, 2008, https://www.bls.gov/news.release/atus2.nr0.htm.

17. YoonKyung Chung, Barbara Downs, Danielle H. Sandler, and Robert Sienkiewicz, "The Parental Gender Earnings Gap in the United States," Center for Economic Studies, United States Census Bureau, January 2017, https://www2.census.gov/ces/wp/2017/CES -WP-17-68.pdf.

18. Shelley J. Correll, Stephen Benard, and In Paik, "Getting a Job: Is There a Motherhood Penalty?," *American Journal of Sociology* 112, no. 5 (March 2007): 1297–1339.

19. Claire Cain Miller, "The 10-Year Baby Window That Is the Key to the Women's Pay Gap," *New York Times*, April 9, 2018, https:// www.nytimes.com/2018/04/09/upshot/the-10-year-baby-window -that-is-the-key-to-the-womens-pay-gap.html.

20. "Down Syndrome," National Down Syndrome Society, 2019, https://www.ndss.org/about-down-syndrome/down-syndrome/.

21. David B. Dunson, Bernardo Colombo, and Donna D. Baird, "Changes with Age in the Level and Duration of Fertility in the Menstrual Cycle," *Human Reproduction* 17, no. 5 (May 2002): 1399–1403, https://academic.oup.com/humrep/article/17/5/1399/845579.

22. Reeta Lampinen, Katri Vehviläinen-Julkunen, and Päivi Kankkunen, "A Review of Pregnancy in Women Over 35 Years of Age," *The Open Nursing Journal* 3 (2009): 33–38, https://www.ncbi.nlm.nih .gov/pmc/articles/PMC2729989/.

23. "Infertility," Office on Women's Health, https://www.womenshealth .gov/a-z-topics/infertility.

24. Heather Murphy, "Lots of Successful Women Are Freezing Their Eggs. But It May Not Be About Their Careers," *New York Times*,

July 3, 2018, https://www.nytimes.com/2018/07/03/health/freezing -eggs-women.html.

25. "Fertility Treatment 2014–2016: Trends and Figures," Human Fertilisation and Embryology Authority, March 2018, https://www.hfea .gov.uk/media/2563/hfea-fertility-trends-and-figures-2017-v2.pdf.

26. R. H. Goldman, C. Racowsky, L. V. Farland, et al. "Predicting the Likelihood of Live Birth for Elective Oocyte Cryopreservation: A Counseling Tool for Physicians and Patients," *Human Reproduction* 32, no. 4 (2017): 853–59.

27. Debarun Majumdar, "Choosing Childlessness: Intentions of Voluntary Childlessness in the United States," *Michigan Sociological Review* 18 (Fall 2004): 108–35.

28. Miller, "Americans Are Having Fewer Babies."

29. Majumdar, "Choosing Childlessness."

30. Ibid.

31. Miller, "Americans Are Having Fewer Babies."

32. Robin Hadley and Terry Hanley, "Involuntarily Childless Men and the Desire for Fatherhood," *Journal of Reproductive and Infant Psychology* 29, no. 1 (February 2011): 56–68.

33. Ibid.

34. Jeffrey M. Jones, "In U.S., 10.2% of LGBT Adults Now Married to Same-Sex Spouse," Gallup, June 22, 2017, https://news.gallup.com /poll/212702/lgbt-adults-married-sex-spouse.aspx.

35. Ibid.

36. "LGBTQ Family Fact Sheet," Family Equality Council, August 2017, https://www2.census.gov/cac/nac/meetings/2017-11/LGBTQ-families-factsheet.pdf.

37. Gary J. Gates, "LGBT Parenting in the United States," The Williams Institute, February 2013, http://williamsinstitute.law.ucla.edu/wp -content/uploads/LGBT-Parenting.pdf.

38. Sarah Jennings, Laura Mellish, Fiona Tasker, et al., "Why Adoption? Gay, Lesbian, and Heterosexual Adoptive Parents' Reproductive Experiences and Reasons for Adoption," *Adoption Quarterly* 17, no. 3

(2014): 205–26, https://www.tandfonline.com/doi/abs/10.1080/109
26755.2014.891549.

39. L. Blake, N. Carone, E. Raffanello, et al., "Gay Fathers' Motivations
for and Feelings about Surrogacy as a Path to Parenthood," *Human
Reproduction* 32, no. 4 (April 2017): 860–67, https://academic.oup
.com/humrep/article/32/4/860/3041131.

40. "Gestational Surrogacy Law Across the United States," Creative
Family Connections, 2016, https://www.creativefamilyconnections
.com/us-surrogacy-law-map/married-same-sex-couples/.

41. "Using a Surrogate Mother: What You Need to Know," WebMD,
https://www.webmd.com/infertility-and-reproduction/guide/using
-surrogate-mother.

42. Leslie Morgan Steiner, *The Baby Chase: How Surrogacy Is Transforming the American Family* (New York: Macmillan, 2013).

43. Ibid.

Chapter Six: Friendship

1. Julianne Holt-Lunstad, Timothy B. Smith, and J. Bradley Layton,
"Social Relationships and Mortality Risk: A Meta-Analytic Review,"
PLOS Medicine July 27, 2010, https://journals.plos.org/plosmedicine
/article?id=10.1371/journal.pmed.1000316.

2. "Cigna U.S. Loneliness Index," Cigna, May 2018, https://www.multivu
.com/players/English/8294451-cigna-us-loneliness-survey/docs
/IndexReport_1524069371598-173525450.pdf.

3. Julie Beck, "How Friendships Change in Adulthood," *The Atlantic*,
October 22, 2015, https://www.theatlantic.com/health/archive
/2015/10/how-friendships-change-over-time-in-adulthood
/411466/.

4. Beverley Fehr, "Friendship Formation," in *Handbook of Relationship Initiation*, ed. Susan Sprecher, Amy Wenzel, and John Harvey
(New York: Taylor & Francis, 2008), 29–54.

5. Ibid.

6. Ibid.

7. Jeffrey A. Hall, "How Many Hours Does It Take to Make a Friend?,"

Journal of Social and Personal Relationships 36, no. 4 (April 1, 2019): 1278–96, https://journals.sagepub.com/doi/full/10.1177/02654 07518761225.

8. See Beck, "How Friendships Change in Adulthood." This article summarizes the academic data on circles of friends.

9. Linton C. Freeman and Claire R. Thompson, "Estimating Acquaintanceship Volume," in *The Small World*, ed. Manfred Kochen (Norwood, NJ: Ablex Publishing Corporation, 1989), 147–58.

10. Russell A. Hill and Robin Ian MacDonald Dunbar, "Social Network Size in Humans," *Human Nature* 14, no. 1 (March 2003): 53–72.

11. Thomas A. DiPrete, Andrew Gelman, Tyler McCormick, et al., "Segregation in Social Networks Based on Acquaintanceship and Trust," *American Journal of Sociology* 116, no. 4 (January 2011): 1234–83.

12. Miller McPherson, Lynn Smith-Lovin, and Matthew E. Brashears, "Social Isolation in America: Changes in Core Discussion Networks over Two Decades," *American Sociological Review* 71, no. 3 (June 1, 2006): 353–75.

13. Henrik Lindberg, "Five Ways to Spend a Thursday," Medium, April 30, 2017, https://towardsdatascience.com/five-ways-to-spend-a -thursday-34432f9ee93e.

14. Kunal Bhattacharya, Asim Ghosh, Daniel Monsivais, et al., "Sex Differences in Social Focus across the Life Cycle in Humans," *Royal Society Open Science* 3, no. 4 (April 2016), https://royalsociety publishing.org/doi/10.1098/rsos.160097.

15. Fatih Karahan and Darius Li, "What Caused the Decline in Interstate Migration in the United States?," Federal Reserve Bank of New York, October 17, 2016, https://libertystreeteconomics.newyorkfed .org/2016/10/what-caused-the-decline-in-interstate-migration-in -the-united-states.html.

16. Michael Bailey, Ruiqing Cao, Theresa Kuchler, and Johannes Stroebel, "The Economic Effects of Social Networks: Evidence from the Housing Market," *Journal of Political Economy* 126, no. 6 (December 2018): 2224–76.

17. Rebecca G. Adams, "Emotional Closeness and Physical Distance between Friends: Implications for Elderly Women Living in Age-Segregated and Age-Integrated Settings," *The International Journal of Aging and Human Development* 22, no. 1 (January 1, 1986): 55–76.

18. Laura L. Carstensen, Bulent Turan, Susanne Scheibe, et al., "Emotional Experience Improves with Age: Evidence Based on over 10 Years of Experience Sampling," *Psychology and Aging* 26, no. 1 (March 2011): 21–33, https://www.ncbi.nlm.nih.gov/pmc/articles/PMC3332527/.

19. "Cigna U.S. Loneliness Index."

20. Josie S. Milligan-Saville, Leona Tan, Aimée Gayed, et al., "Workplace Mental Health Training for Managers and Its Effect on Sick Leave in Employees: A Cluster Randomised Controlled Trial," *The Lancet Psychiatry* 4, no. 11 (November 1, 2017): 850–58, https://www.thelancet.com/journals/lanpsy/article/PIIS2215-0366(17)30372-3/fulltext.

21. Arthur C. Brooks, "How Loneliness Is Tearing America Apart," *New York Times*, November 23, 2018, https://www.nytimes.com/2018/11/23/opinion/loneliness-political-polarization.html.

22. Julianne Holt-Lunstad, Timothy B. Smith, Mark Baker, et al., "Loneliness and Social Isolation as Risk Factors for Mortality: A Meta-analytic Review," *Perspectives on Psychological Science* 10, no. 2 (March 2015): 227–37.

23. Ibid.

24. "Beyond Happiness: Thriving," AARP, June 4, 2012, https://www.aarp.org/content/dam/aarp/research/surveys_statistics/general/2012/Beyond-Happiness-Thriving-AARP.pdf.

25. William J. Chopik, "Associations Among Relational Values, Support, Health, and Well-Being Across the Adult Lifespan," *Personal Relationships* 24, no. 2 (2017): 408–22.

26. Mark S. Granovetter, "The Strength of Weak Ties," *American Journal of Sociology* 78, no. 6 (May 1973): 1360–80, https://www.cs.cmu.edu/~jure/pub/papers/granovetter73ties.pdf.

27. Gillian M. Sandstrom and Elizabeth W. Dunn, "Social Interactions and Well-Being: The Surprising Power of Weak Ties," *Personality and Social Psychology Bulletin* 40, no. 7 (July 1, 2014): 910–22.

28. Juliet Ruth Helen Wakefield, Fabio Sani, Vishnu Madhok, et al., "The Relationship Between Group Identification and Satisfaction with Life in a Cross-Cultural Community Sample," *Journal of Happiness Studies* 18, no. 3 (June 2017): 785–807, https://link.springer.com /article/10.1007/s10902-016-9735-z.

29. Sylvia A. Morelli, Desmond C. Ong, Rucha Makati, et al., "Empathy and Well-Being Correlate with Centrality in Different Social Networks," *Proceedings of the National Academy of Sciences of the United States of America* 114, no. 37 (September 12, 2017): 9843–47, https://www.pnas.org/content/114/37/9843.

30. Karen D. Ersche, Tsen-Vei Lim, Laetitia H. E. Ward, et al., "Creature of Habit: A Self-Report Measure of Habitual Routines and Automatic Tendencies in Everyday Life," *Personality and Individual Differences* 116 (October 2017): 73–85, https://www.ncbi.nlm.nih.gov /pmc/articles/PMC5473478/.

31. Alex Williams, "Why Is It Hard to Make Friends over 30?," *New York Times*, July 13, 2012, https://www.nytimes.com/2012/07/15 /fashion/the-challenge-of-making-friends-as-an-adult.html.

32. Brené Brown, "The Power of Vulnerability," TED, June 2010, https:// www.ted.com/talks/brene_brown_on_vulnerability/transcript.

Chapter Seven: Politics

1. Marilyn Berger, "Suharto, Ex-Dictator of Indonesia, Dead at 86," *New York Times*, January 27, 2008, https://www.nytimes.com/2008 /01/27/world/asia/27iht-suharto.1.9521658.html.

2. R. J. Reinhart, "Global Warming Age Gap: Younger Americans Most Worried," Gallup, May 11, 2018, https://news.gallup.com/poll /234314/global-warming-age-gap-younger-americans-worried .aspx.

3. Nick Davis, "Millennials Are More Likely to Oppose Racism," Data for Progress, January 29, 2019, https://www.dataforprogress.org /blog/2019/1/29/unpacking-millennials-racial-attitudes.

4. David Brancaccio and Janet Nguyen, "Where Millennials Stand on Immigration," *Marketplace*, National Public Radio, February 5, 2018, https://www.marketplace.org/2018/02/05/where-millennials -stand-immigration/.

5. Richard Fry, "Millennials Approach Baby Boomers as America's Largest Generation in the Electorate," Pew Research Center, April 3, 2018, https://www.pewresearch.org/fact-tank/2018/04/03 /millennials-approach-baby-boomers-as-largest-generation-in-u-s -electorate/.

6. Thom File, "Voting in America: A Look at the 2016 Presidential Election," United States Census Bureau, May 10, 2017, https:// www.census.gov/newsroom/blogs/random-samplings/2017/05 /voting_in_america.html.

7. Jordan Misra, "Behind the 2018 U.S. Midterm Election Turnout," United States Census Bureau, April 23, 2019, https://www.census .gov/library/stories/2019/04/behind-2018-united-states-midterm -election-turnout.html.

8. Kim Parker, Nikki Graf, and Ruth Igielnik, "Generation Z Looks a Lot like Millennials on Key Social and Political Issues," Pew Research Center, January 17, 2019, https://www.pewsocialtrends.org /2019/01/17/generation-z-looks-a-lot-like-millennials-on-key-social -and-political-issues/.

9. Shiva Maniam and Samantha Smith, "A Wider Partisan and Ideological Gap between Younger, Older Generations," Pew Research Center, March 20, 2017, https://www.pewresearch.org/fact -tank/2017/03/20/a-wider-partisan-and-ideological-gap-between -younger-older-generations/.

10. "For Most Trump Voters, 'Very Warm' Feelings for Him Endured," Pew Research Center, August 9, 2018, https://www.people-press .org/2018/08/09/for-most-trump-voters-very-warm-feelings-for -him-endured/.

11. Markus Prior, "News vs. Entertainment: How Increasing Media Choice Widens Gaps in Political Knowledge and Turnout," *American Journal of Political Science* 49, no. 3 (2005): 577–92, https:// onlinelibrary.wiley.com/doi/abs/10.1111/j.1540-5907.2005.00143.x.

12. Donald P. Green, Bradley Palmquist, and Eric Schickler, *Partisan*

Hearts and Minds: Political Parties and the Social Identities of Voters (New Haven, CT: Yale University Press, 2004).

13. Ibid., chap. 3.

14. Marc Meredith, "Persistence in Political Participation," *Quarterly Journal of Political Science* 4, no. 3 (October 2009): 187–209.

15. Leonardo Bursztyn, Davide Cantoni, David Y. Yang, et al., "Persistent Political Engagement: Social Interactions and the Dynamics of Protest Movements," working paper June 2019, https://home.uchicago.edu/bursztyn/Persistent_Political_Engagement_July2019.pdf.

16. John B. Holbein and D. Sunshine Hillygus, "Making Young Voters: The Impact of Preregistration on Youth Turnout," *American Journal of Political Science* 60, no. 2 (April 2016): 364–82.

17. Ibid., 365.

18. Benjamin Highton and Raymond E. Wolfinger, "The First Seven Years of the Political Life Cycle," *American Journal of Political Science* 45, no. 1 (January 2001): 202–09.

19. John M. Strate, Charles J. Parrish, Charles D. Elder, and Coit Ford, "Life Span Civic Development and Voting Participation," *The American Political Science Review* 83, no. 2 (June 1989): 443–64.

20. "Current Population Survey Data for Social, Economic, and Health Research," IPUMS-CPS, 2018, https://cps.ipums.org.

21. "Are Millennials the Screwed Generation?," Daily Beast, April 24, 2017, https://www.thedailybeast.com/videos/2012/07/16/are-millennials-the-screwed-generation.

22. Alan S. Gerber and Donald P. Green, "The Effects of Canvassing, Telephone Calls, and Direct Mail on Voter Turnout: A Field Experiment," *American Political Science Review* 94, no. 3 (September 2000): 653–63.

23. Alan S. Gerber, Donald P. Green, and Christopher W. Larimer, "Social Pressure and Voter Turnout: Evidence from a Large-Scale Field Experiment," *American Political Science Review* 102, no. 1 (February 2008): 33–48, https://isps.yale.edu/sites/default/files/publication/2012/12/ISPS08-001.pdf.

24. David W. Nickerson, "Hunting the Elusive Young Voter," *Journal of Political Marketing* 5, no. 3 (2006): 47–69.

25. Ibid.

26. Davide Cantoni, David Y. Yang, Noam Yuchtman, and Y. Jane Zhang, "Protests as Strategic Games: Experimental Evidence from Hong Kong's Antiauthoritarian Movement," *The Quarterly Journal of Economics* 134, no. 2 (May 2019): 1021–77, https://academic.oup.com/qje/article/134/2/1021/5298503.

27. Gwyneth H. McClendon, "Social Esteem and Participation in Contentious Politics: A Field Experiment at an LGBT Pride Rally," *American Journal of Political Science* 58, no. 2 (April 2014): 279–90.

Chapter Eight: Faith

1. Michael Lipka, "Millennials Increasingly Are Driving Growth of 'Nones,'" Pew Research Center, May 12, 2015, https://www.pewresearch.org/fact-tank/2015/05/12/millennials-increasingly-are-driving-growth-of-nones/.

2. "Faith in Flux," Pew Research Center, April 27, 2009, https://www.pewforum.org/2009/04/27/faith-in-flux/.

3. Michael Lipka, "A Closer Look at America's Rapidly Growing Religious 'Nones,'" Pew Research Center, May 13, 2015, https://www.pewresearch.org/fact-tank/2015/05/13/a-closer-look-at-americas-rapidly-growing-religious-nones/.

4. James W. Fowler, *Stages of Faith: The Psychology of Human Development and the Quest for Meaning* (New York: HarperOne, 1995).

5. Betsy Cooper, Daniel Cox, Rachel Lienisch, and Robert P. Jones, "Exodus: Why Americans Are Leaving Religion—and Why They're Unlikely to Come Back," Public Religion Research Institute, September 22, 2016, https://www.prri.org/research/prri-rns-poll-nones-atheist-leaving-religion/.

6. Becka A. Alper, "Millennials Are Less Religious than Older Americans, but Just as Spiritual," Pew Research Center, November 23, 2015, https://www.pewresearch.org/fact-tank/2015/11/23/millennials-are-less-religious-than-older-americans-but-just-as-spiritual/.

7. Becka A. Alper, "Why America's 'Nones' Don't Identify with a Religion," Pew Research Center, August 8, 2018, https://www.pewresearch.org/fact-tank/2018/08/08/why-americas-nones-dont-identify-with-a-religion/.

8. Cooper et al., "Exodus."

9. David Masci, "Q&A: Why Millennials Are Less Religious than Older Americans," Pew Research Center, January 8, 2016, https://www.pewresearch.org/fact-tank/2016/01/08/qa-why-millennials-are-less-religious-than-older-americans/.

10. Cooper et al., "Exodus."

11. Jeff Diamant and Besheer Mohamed, "Black Millennials Are More Religious than Other Millennials," Pew Research Center, July 20, 2018, https://www.pewresearch.org/fact-tank/2018/07/20/black-millennials-are-more-religious-than-other-millennials/.

12. Catherine E. Ross, "Religion and Psychological Distress," *Journal for the Scientific Study of Religion* 29, no. 2 (1990): 236–45.

13. Sarvada Chandra Tiwari, "Loneliness: A Disease?," *Indian Journal of Psychiatry* 55, no. 4 (2013): 320–22, http://www.indianjpsychiatry.org/article.asp?issn=0019-5545;year=2013;volume=55;issue=4;spage=320;epage=322;aulast=Tiwari.

14. "Why Americans Go to Religious and Church Services," Pew Research Center, August 1, 2018, https://www.pewforum.org/2018/08/01/why-americans-go-to-religious-services/.

15. Cooper et al., "Exodus."

16. "U.S. Public Becoming Less Religious," Pew Research Center, November 3, 2015, https://www.pewforum.org/2015/11/03/u-s-public-becoming-less-religious/.

17. Alper, "Millennials Are Less Religious than Older Americans, but Just as Spiritual."

18. Ibid.

19. Ibid.

20. Daniel Cox, "Are White Evangelicals Sacrificing the Future in Search of the Past?," FiveThirtyEight, January 24, 2018, https://fivethirtyeight.com/features/are-white-evangelicals-sacrificing-the-future-in-search-of-the-past/.

21. "Does Having Children Make Parents More Active Churchgoers?," Barna, May 24, 2010, https://www.barna.com/research/does-having-children-make-parents-more-active-churchgoers/.

22. *America's Changing Religious Landscape*, Pew Research Center, May 12, 2015, https://www.pewforum.org/wp-content/uploads /sites/7/2015/05/RLS-08-26-full-report.pdf, chap 2.

23. "Faith in Flux."

24. Cooper et al., "Exodus."

ABOUT THE AUTHOR

ELIZABETH SEGRAN spent her childhood in Brussels, Paris, Singapore, and Jakarta. She moved to New York to attend Columbia University, then went on to get a PhD from the University of California, Berkeley, women's studies and Indian literature. She's a senior staff writer at the business magazine *Fast Company*, where she covers fashion, sustainability, and design. Her work has been published in a wide range of publications, including the *Atlantic*, the *Nation*, *Foreign Policy*, and the *New Republic*. She lives in Boston with her husband and daughter.